The Purposeful PhD

The Purposeful PhD

Aligning Your Career with Your Purpose, Values, and Impact

Rebecca Paradiso de Sayu

The Purposeful PhD
Aligning Your Career with Your Purpose, Values, and Impact

Copyright © 2021 by Rebecca Paradiso de Sayu

Published by Gentle Autumn Press
Madison, Wisconsin, United States

Interior Design by Kimberly Martin, Jera Publishing
Cover Design by Jason Orr, Jera Publishing
Author Photograph, Twig & Olive Photography

All rights reserved. No part of this book may be reproduced or transmitted in any form or by any means without written permission of the author. Requests should be sent to info@thepurposefulphd.com.

Bulk order discounts are available.
Please contact orders@thepurposefulphd.com.

ISBN 978-1-7378872-0-1

Subjects: Career Development | Professional Development | Higher Education | Collective Wellbeing

Printed in the United States of America

Dedication

To my parents, whose untimely passing taught me that there is no better moment than right now to follow your truth, even when you don't know where it will lead. In uncertainty, there is also magic.

Contents

A Note to Graduate School Administrators & Faculty i

Introduction 1

Section 1   Your PhD Journey 5

Section 2   Honor Your Purpose 19

Section 3   Shape Your Life Around Your Values 37

Section 4   Make an Impact 59

Section 5   A New Way Forward 81

References 91

Acknowledgements 95

Biography 99

A Note to Graduate School Administrators & Faculty

If you have recommended or purchased this book for your students/trainees, you no doubt recognize that the professional and personal support needs of PhD students and postdocs are changing. With the unprecedented number of PhD graduates poised to enter the job market, the need for resources that help navigate career choices is growing exponentially. And perhaps even more importantly, PhDs at any place along their academic and professional journeys want to be seen and encouraged to pursue careers that align with their sense of purpose without shame or fear of perceived failure.

Graduate and postdoctoral training programs have an opportunity to transform the culture of higher education by nurturing the diversity of students' values and centering their wellbeing. Part of this shift places responsibility upon leadership to normalize and validate a host of career paths that add value to society.

Sharing this workbook with prospective and current PhD students and postdocs signals your commitment to their personal and professional development and support for how they make meaning of the degree in their own lives. On behalf of all of us, *thank you.*

Introduction

FORGET WHAT YOU'VE been told about career options for PhD holders. Forget what you think you know about the inevitability of the tenure track. Even forget what you've been telling yourself about what life will look like after you finish the degree. What you've learned is one version of what's possible, and there are so many more...

What you probably haven't been encouraged to explore is what it means to create a life in service to *you*: your path, your joy, and your purpose. That's where I step in.

The Purposeful PhD acknowledges the fears and questions you might have when you think about your future with a PhD, and it offers support along the path. To do that, I weave together different ways of knowing — research, creativity, and self-wisdom — and I invite you to slow down, reconnect to your purpose, and consider how a career can align with the life you want.

So many of us want to be more. So many of us hunger to discover who we might become together.

—Margaret Wheatley & Myron Kellner-Rogers,
Co-Founders of the Berkana Institute

You'll receive advice from *real* people[*] who have used their PhDs to impact society in deeply satisfying ways and learn tips for translating your expertise across industries — academia, government, nonprofit, and business.

This is the only professional development workbook for PhDs that is completely career-agnostic. No hierarchies, no favoritism, no nonsense.

What does that mean? I believe that *any* career that aligns with your purpose and values is valid and refuse to hold one above another. I celebrate policymakers, data scientists, tenure track professors, entrepreneurs, and stay-at-home parents. A PhD will enhance whichever path you choose.

It might feel like the connection between PhD and purpose is unclear. That makes sense. For so long, academia has drawn a narrow line from the PhD directly to the tenure track. So, when you start thinking about other career choices, you might only have a vague idea of how relevant the degree can be. That is, until now.

Whether you've just started thinking about getting a PhD, are in the throes of grad school, working on a postdoc, or thinking of a career change, allow yourself to reimagine how a PhD can support your sense of purpose and enhance career opportunities no matter the path you choose.

What I'm offering you is an open invitation to dream — because, if the last time you really asked yourself what you wanted to be when you grew up was when you were a child — chances are good that those dreams have changed. Now is the time to think about a career that resonates with *you* — the person you are today — and what you want from your life.

How to Use this Workbook

In each section, you'll learn about potential careers, read stories of PhDs flourishing across industries, review tips for translating your experience

---

[*] Job titles of PhD professionals highlighted throughout this book reflect their roles at the time of writing and may have since changed. As shorthand, I'll refer to professionals who have attained a PhD as "PhDs."

and expertise into jobs that align with your purpose, values, and lifestyle goals, confront your fears about the realities of a shifting job market, and get practical advice on how to take steps toward *your* ideal professional future. At the end of each section, you'll find ideas and recommendations specific to different stages of PhD life: pre-PhD, current PhD students, and postdocs/PhD graduates. Some of these formats will resonate with you, and some may not. Use the parts that serve you as you envision the thriving professional you want to be.

SECTION 1

Your PhD Journey

You Belong

I **WANT TO SET** the groundwork before we go any farther. You belong. I mean *you*. No matter who you are, where you come from, whether you are the first in your family to get any kind of degree, whether there have — or haven't — been other people in your program who look or think like you, you matter.

Everything that you are is worthy of pursuing doctoral education. You already have what it takes to earn your PhD and land the career of your choosing. I'm not talking about the skills and expertise, that comes later for everyone. I'm talking about the innate brilliance, the credibility, and the resilience that you have at this very moment.

Honor the space between no longer and not yet.
—Nancy Levin, Author & Master Life Coach

The central tenets of my work are racial equity, inclusion, and collective wellbeing for *all*. In this book, you'll see representation of PhDs from a diversity of racial and ethnic backgrounds, as well as a disproportionately large number of women. This is not a flaw in the design; it *is* the design. Representation matters. I hope you see faces that remind you that there are people ready and waiting to support your journey and who get it from a deep place of knowing.

I wholeheartedly believe that to move the needle on countless social, political, and economic issues, society demands a myriad of unique perspectives. Without you, we are lacking, and not the other way around. And it is incumbent upon systems — including higher education — to prioritize the wellbeing of learners for the benefit of all. You've got this, and I'm wholeheartedly cheering for your success.

Explore Your Options

Gina Gallego-López, Veterinary Sciences

"Students need to explore different career paths. Try an internship in the private sector to figure out if you like it. Teach a class to see if you like it. Prototype different career scenarios. This way, you can get a bigger picture of your opportunities and choose what works for you."

All About the Fit

PhDs are socialized that going on the tenure track job market is like trying to find parking on the busiest shopping day of the year. You find a "spot" and make it work.

For some people, pursuing the tenure track will feel like the SUV pictured on the next page — crammed in a space that doesn't feel right. Others will find it comfortable. Who knows, they might have arrived at the parking lot in a mini car! In all seriousness though, there's no right or wrong here. It truly is a matter of personal fit.

The problem is that so often, PhDs are only prepared with the tools, skills, and mindsets for one path — the tenure track — no matter their career inclination. And this lack of preparedness, along with any feelings of shame, guilt, or doubt, can leave PhDs wondering where they went wrong.

My hope is that as you make your way through this workbook, you'll embrace the idea that some career options work for you, and some don't. That's okay.

If you are struggling with the question of whether the tenure track fits, know that I have abundant compassion for your journey. That was me.

Grieving the loss of what you'd assumed would be your professional identity doesn't make you dramatic, and honoring your sense of purpose isn't fluff. Tuning into yourself can lead your life in directions you might never have imagined. And no matter where you land, I want you to know that your path is worthy.

If feelings of remorse creep up, ask yourself why you wanted to be a professor in the first place. No doubt, it's an exciting and honorable path, but what are the reasons that led *you* to that decision? Is it your love of research or teaching? Is it the prestige of being a professor? Or is it because it's the path you were taught to revere? Could you do the things you love in a different career or industry?

How Did We Get Here?

Since 1958, the National Center for Science and Engineering Statistics, Survey of Earned Doctorates (SED)[1] has tracked data from all PhD recipients in the United States (U.S.).

In that time, the number of PhDs graduating from U.S. universities has soared. According to the most recent SED data, in 2019, 55,703 PhDs graduated from U.S. colleges and universities compared to 8,773 in 1958 when the survey began. That's a whopping 535% increase!

Presumably, universities employ more tenure track professors today than in the 50s, leading to an increased demand. Yet the influx of PhDs has far outpaced today's staffing needs, especially in light of hiring freezes and other administrative uncertainties arising from the COVID-19 pandemic.

The Emotional Work
Julia Gilden,
Biomedical Science

"Some of my most important work in grad school was emotional. I had to examine what assumptions about myself were keeping me in academia and process what it meant to let go."

How Many Grads Take the Tenure Track?

While there is variation across fields of study, SED data from 2019 reported that across all fields, 63% of PhD graduates had definitive plans — employment or postdoctoral studies (i.e., postdocs) — **at the time of graduation.** Per the survey, postdocs are classified as training positions, rather than employees.

Of those graduates with definitive employment at the time of graduation, 41.3% went into academia. Within this segment, 42% reported tenure track faculty positions, while the remaining 58% reported other academic roles such as non-tenure-track faculty, administrators, scientists, outreach specialists, etc.

When it's all said and done, only **7%** all PhD graduates have a tenure track professorship lined up at the time of graduation. Let that sink in...

These data represent averages across all disciplines. However, there is variation across fields when it comes to percentage of PhDs with definitive career plans at the time of graduation, type of postgraduation plans, employment sector, etc. Additionally, some PhDs will accept tenure track positions after graduation, including a portion of graduates who took postdocs before seeking employment. Among postdocs, however, the percentage that receive and accept tenure track positions is low[2].

The Power of Choice

Given these odds, you might be wondering, *"How am I ever going to get a professor job?"*

It's counterintuitive, but what if you reframed the situation around the *power of choice*? Rather than fighting the limitations of a saturated tenure track market, imagine the boundless opportunities that arise when you indulge all your possibilities.

Note

My coaching clients (especially postdocs) have taught me that having so many career choices can also be stressful. The paradox of choice — too many options, leading to overwhelm and feeling stuck — is real. As I will talk about in the next section, part of a purpose-driven job search is narrowing your choices to only those that align with the life you are trying to create. When you do that, the total number of options is inconsequential.

Admittedly, this is a hard sell. My options weren't obvious to me *at all* in grad school. You might feel that way too. It was not until I graduated and worked in the academic, nonprofit, government, and private sectors that I witnessed countless ways a career can unfold when you have a PhD in your back pocket. With your training, an open mind, and an open heart, the career options ahead of you are virtually limitless. You're going to need to trust me on this one.

When you embrace the "radical" idea that your degree — and your career — is yours to create, you unlock a future you might never have thought was possible.

PhD Superpowers

Graduate and postdoctoral training is designed to develop your analytic thinking, advanced research capabilities, and a host of topical expertise. I call these your **PhD Superpowers**! In academia, you're surrounded by people who have similar gifts, so you might not realize that your Superpowers are actually quite extraordinary. To be clear, a PhD is *not* a prerequisite for any of the Superpowers, but they are easily overlooked if you assume that everyone has them. Here are some examples:

- **Research:** A fraction of jobs require advanced scientific research skills, but nearly all jobs need people who can collect and assess information — anything from locating the perfect conference venue to evaluating different computer software options to making company policy recommendations based on what has worked for similar organizations. You might assume that anyone with basic internet skills can get the job done, but that's not always the case.

    A PhD colleague of mine joked that in her family, she is *the* go-to person for Google searches. In 5 minutes, she can find *and* synthesize the same information that could take others an hour to find. And this is true in organizations too. Your ability to judge the quality and credibility of information quickly is not a skill that everyone has.

- **Critical Thinking:** The ability to identify a problem, evaluate information and prototype — or test out — potential solutions is highly regarded across industries. As a result of your PhD and post-doctoral training, you'll master the art of critical thinking and will intuitively know how to solve a problem, even if you've never been in the same situation before. You'll also know how to identify people and information that can lead you in the right direction rather than immediately needing to defer to your supervisor for the answer.

- **Clear Communication:** A dissertation defense is largely about making a clear, convincing argument that your research is accurate and valuable. How you prove your point requires strong written (dissertation) and spoken (oral defense) communication.

Of course, you don't need a PhD to be a good writer. However, graduate training provides ample opportunities to hone your craft. If you've already completed graduate coursework, you have likely received papers with feedback literally *everywhere*. That's where the learning happens — and keeps

Change the System from Within
Atiera Coleman, Sociology

Atiera's PhD in Sociology — along with personal understanding of the struggle underrepresented students experience in higher ed — made her the ideal candidate for her role as Associate Dean of Student Success, Equity, and Community Division at a small liberal arts college.

Atiera shared, "I began my equity work when I realized that some of the obstacles for students were at the college institutional level."

By relaying her experiences and advancing diversity and inclusion, Atiera has been able to promote a more equitable campus experience for her students.

happening — over and over again. Through the course of writing dozens of papers, presenting at conferences, and preparing articles for publication, you learn how to communicate, and this is a prized skill.

Know that you will likely have some unlearning to do when it comes to communication if you leave the academy. The ease you feel with spitting out complex jargon may be unnecessarily technical for the audiences your organization wants to reach. A consumer audience is very different from an academic audience, for example.

- **Self-Direction:** Crafting and defending your dissertation is the ultimate test of self-motivation, drive, and perseverance. You design the research process, you carry it out, and you synthesize the findings. Reliance on yourself to make progress is the name of the game. If you take a management position — or any job that requires decision-making responsibilities — you'll quickly see how your ability to act with agency and to trust your intuition matters to getting the job done.

During a group coaching session, a postdoc shared that at a recent conference, one of the speakers — a PhD working in the private sector — made a comment that left a lasting impression. He said, "I view someone with a PhD as someone with the ability to learn quickly. I am less concerned with their area of specialty and more with the fact that they can synthesize information and test out new ideas, even when the subject is completely outside of their field."

Another participant added, "I was talking with a recruiting manager about what makes PhDs competitive for jobs in industry. He told me that he does not expect recent PhD grads to know everything about working in his company. That's okay. That's something he can teach them. What he has seen time and time again, however, is their potential to leverage broader competencies (i.e., Superpowers) that add significant value to the organization."

A Personal Shift

You'll come to find that in addition to your Superpowers, a PhD can have a transformative effect on how you see yourself.

After successfully jumping through the hoops that grad school threw their way — every class, every revision, every unexpected turn — many PhDs and postdocs tell me that the confidence they gained by putting themselves out there, taking risks, and being okay with making mistakes, is unparalleled.

The awareness that you might not have every answer, but that you can figure it out, is exhilarating. And this helps battle the pains of impostor syndrome when you're in unknown territory.

As one colleague shared with me, "I don't feel stupid anymore if I need to ask someone to explain something a different way, or if I have questions. I know I'm not stupid — I have a PhD!"

But why do you need a PhD to feel confident, to ask questions, and to take risks? The simple answer is **you don't**.

You might be thinking:

> *If I don't want a tenure track job, then why should I get a PhD instead of a Master's or another degree? You just said I don't need a PhD to feel confident and smart!*

At the end of the day, the answer to that question will come down to any number of personal reasons — *I love to learn!* — to the practical — *I just finished my master's and the job market sucks, might as well keep going!* — to the reality — *The job that I want requires a PhD*. And on and on.

Ironically, my answer didn't come until I completed the degree. Suddenly I felt like a different person — a more confident and bolder person! Much to my surprise, this new identity felt in many ways as transformative as becoming a parent. Not because I valued the experiences in the same way, but because there was a distinct *Before and After* feeling. How you will feel with your degree in hand, of course, will be very personal, and the path to get there, your very own.

TOP TIPS: STEP ASIDE, EGO!

One of the most important pieces of advice I received in grad school was *not* to limit my job search to those that require a PhD. At the time, that suggestion didn't make sense.

My ego fooled me into believing that whatever job I chose would need my fancy new credentials. *Those* were the jobs I was going to pursue. It turns out that lots of positions outside of academia don't require a PhD. A real light-bulb moment happened in grad school when I realized that many of the PhDs who had the kinds of careers I wanted worked for organizations that didn't require the degree but where they could immediately add value and feel satisfied.

It wasn't until I separated my ego from my career search — and stopped insisting that a job require my niche expertise — that I realized the profundity of my choices.

Many PhDs and postdocs I talk with struggle because they want a career that rewards their specialized knowledge and skills. This is one of the reasons why the tenure track is so appealing. By design, professors are rewarded for their unique contributions to a narrow area of their field.

Yet many organizations prize critical thinking, complex information processing, and clear communication — remember the PhD Superpowers? Not every job will use your skills in the same way, and none are less worthy of your consideration. Don't let assumptions of what you think someone with a PhD should be doing deter you from a career that aligns with your purpose.

Nearly every PhD I've met says the degree has brought value whether it was required for the position or not. Having it often offers unique advantages, for example, putting you on the fast track to promotion, starting at a higher-level position or salary, or having more autonomy.

The Ultimate Reframe

In light of COVID-19 — and intensified economic and social unrest, climate change and shifts in political power — the world needs more people with keen critical thinking and problem-solving skills, trusted intuition, top-notch research abilities, and persistence in the face of uncertainty.

While it's tempting to see our shifting reality as yet another career barrier, what if you approached it as *the ultimate moment* to make an impact? What if instead of adopting a scarcity mindset — focusing on the dearth of tenure track positions, made worse by hiring freezes and job cuts — you reframed the situation as one of abundant opportunities?

What if the risk of waiting for the "perfect" job was greater than taking a different path to be a part of a global transformation?

With your PhD, you are well positioned to create innovative solutions needed to navigate uncharted territory across sectors and across the globe. No matter your discipline — engineering, psychology, biology, economics, or nursing — you can play a critical role in reshaping society.

And know this: the career choices you make today will not define you for the rest of your professional life. No job is so permanent that you can't try something different at another point. The most important thing is to get started.

Ideal Career Traits Activity

What does your ideal career look like? What job would make you excited about getting up in the morning? What's your ideal workspace - is it quiet or noisy, cluttered or clean, remote or on site? What kind of projects would you enjoy tackling? What kind of team do you want to join?

Have you asked yourself these questions? If not, why? Is it because the PhD feels like an automatic road to the tenure track? Is it because you've been too busy keeping up with grad school or your postdoc to stop and consider? Or maybe it's because you thought you didn't have a choice. With these questions in mind, let's review the following activity:

Below, take a few minutes to brainstorm — without barriers — your ideal career. You can describe characteristics of the job, skills you'd like to use, activities you'd like to perform, or aspects of the organizational culture that matter most to you. Don't over think this or get too particular, for example, listing specific job titles. Just let your mind go where it pleases.

_____

_____

_____

_____

_____

_____

_____

_____

_____

_____

_____

_____

_____

When you're done, share your ideas with a trusted friend or partner, or reflect for a minute on what you've imagined for yourself.

Next, rank your ideal traits in order of importance. Like finding the perfect apartment or partner, finding the ideal career will involve some sticking to your guns and compromise. Be realistic and choose one or two "must haves." A job that meets *all* your career dreams might not exist, and that's okay. This is not about perfection; it's about being clear about what matters most to you.

Periodically update your ideal career traits based on new information and experiences. Review the PhD career profiles provided throughout the workbook. Can you picture yourself in any of the jobs described? Would that job fulfill any of your ideal career traits?

Once you have your ideal career traits list, you'll stop asking yourself "Do I have what it takes to land this job?" and start thinking, "Does this job offer some of the characteristics that matter most to *me*?"

SECTION 2

Honor Your Purpose

WHEN YOU THINK about the life you want to live, how does it look? What sparks your curiosity? Energizes you to keep going on hard days? Makes you feel satisfied that your time is well spent? The answers to these questions speak to your **purpose**.

Purpose is powerful. In their 2018 study of the relationship between purpose, stress, and wellbeing, Dr. Patrick Hill and colleagues[3] share that having a sense of purpose increases your physical and mental health, sense of satisfaction, and boosts motivation to keep going when you feel bored, frustrated, or discouraged. Purpose gives you a sense of hope.

When you are deciding on the next steps, next jobs, next careers, further education, you should rather find purpose than a job or a career. Purpose crosses disciplines. Purpose is an essential element of you. It is the reason you are on the planet at this particular time in history.
—Chadwick Boseman, American Actor

A sense of purpose feeds the core intention of everything we do and who we want to be.

Why does knowing your purpose matter to your career? Isn't it a personal thing?

Many Western cultures have largely managed to unlearn the deep connection between our personal and professional lives. Attempting to protect our time and to create boundaries, the rise of "work-life balance" has created a false dichotomy between the two. That's not to say that every aspect of professional life will perfectly align with our personal lives. It is to say, however, that what stirs your spirit *matters* when it comes to deciding on your career.

In an age of unlimited access to information — and with so many career options — your purpose acts as a bridge between the person you want to be and the career you pursue. Being clear about your purpose can help narrow your career options.

Ignite Passion in Others
Regina Williams, Special Education Leadership

"During undergrad, I discovered a passion for working with people with disabilities. I was taken aback by the disproportionate number of Black boys in special education for reasons that had less to do with intellectual ability and more to do with lacking resources to meet their basic needs. In addition to being a special education teacher, I work as adjunct faculty because I want to pass on my skill set and ignite passion in future educators."

Narrow my options?! I don't have enough options to start narrowing the field!

I hear this a lot. Your career options are considerably more abundant than you might think. Once you wrap your head around the many ways your life could go with a PhD, you'll want to add filters to help focus your direction.

Paradoxically, another frequent question is:

I'm overwhelmed by my choices! I have so many degrees and experiences that I can't possibly find a career that makes use of everything!

That may be true. Some PhD students and postdocs have had several professional lives — for example, in law, business, medicine and science — before starting the degree.

For this group, the same advice applies: Anchor your job search to your **sense of purpose** as you explore the options. Some jobs will use one set of your talents, others will leverage completely different ones. You aren't settling — nor will you be less competitive in the future — if you focus on a subset of your skills. On the contrary, testing out careers that emphasize various aspects of your expertise offers unique insight into what different industries value.

It's a myth that you are 'locked' in a specific career direction because your current job requires some parts of your training and not others.

The age of staying in the same career for a lifetime is over. You will have opportunities to prototype various jobs, which could mean trying out a job for a year and then deciding it's not the right match. In other words, your career choices aren't permanent.

Take the opportunity to learn the context and values embedded within different industries and particular companies. Everything you observe will help to inform your next career move and deepen your understanding of how various organizations work.

When you embrace the enormity of your career choices, you'll find you have freedom to curate a life that aligns with your deepest sense of self.

One of the best pieces of advice I received was to try out careers in the business, government, nonprofit, and academic sectors so that I knew which environments resonated with my values. Heeding that advice has given me a competitive edge in understanding how different organizations operate and crystalized the aspects of professional life that are most important to me.

Contribute to Science Outside of the Academy

Michael Killoran, Biomolecular Chemistry

As a senior scientist for a biotech manufacturer, Michael has an exciting career. His interdisciplinary team is embedded within the company's Research and Development (R&D) Department where they focus on researching new technologies rather than product design. Working in industry has afforded them the ability to take on riskier, long-term projects, and pursue novel solutions that address unmet needs in the scientific community.

In his role, Michael champions ideas for new solutions and has freedom to explore proof-of-concept experiments that justify resources for promising research. Some of the topics he has tackled include: engineering complex diagnostic systems, machine learning, and visualizing protein interactions for studying disease.

Describing the highlights of the job, Michael shared, "My work keeps me incredibly engaged. It's a constant, but exciting, challenge. Our team has high expectations and often experiences the failures of pushing the state-of-the-art in biotechnology. But when we're successful, it's rewarding to know we are contributing to the company's progress and offering researchers around the world with tools to do amazing things, even beyond what we had envisioned."

Lastly, know that if you decide to pursue a non-tenure-track career, this doesn't signal the end of your academic life. There are so many ways to stay involved with universities by joining advisory boards, participating on dissertation committees, partnering with university colleagues for funding opportunities or to publish research, and of course, taking any number of academic career roles such as advisors, administrators, and curriculum consultants, just to name a few.

If you fear losing the chance to be a part of cutting-edge research, know that across sectors, research teams are charged with developing new technologies, testing groundbreaking solutions, and advancing the scientific community in real time.

Design Thinking

In their *New York Times* bestselling book, *Designing Your Life: How to Build a Well-Lived Joyful Life*[4], Silicon Valley innovators and Stanford educators Bill Burnett and Dave Evans say that the goal of life is one that has *consistency*. Consistency, they argue, is a connection between who you are, what you believe, and what you do.

They describe *design thinking* as a process for creative problem solving that helps users to check-in with the beliefs that shape conscious and unconscious thoughts. For example, design thinking prompts questions like:

> *What, specifically, are my favorite aspects of my studies or work that I'd like to explore in a PhD program?*

> *Does a PhD complement the activities I like to do, for example, learning and research?*

> *If I could create the ideal career, what skills would I need?*

> *What does a day in the life of a professor or nonprofit president really look like?*

Whether you connect with the idea of life consistency — or, as I like to describe it, finding alignment between your sense of purpose, your values, and the impact you want to have on society — the point is this: To find fulfillment in your career, start by being honest about who you are, what you enjoy, and the conditions that support this version of you.

And, as always, be mindful of how much you let others shape the vision for your life.

Purpose is the place where your deep gladness meets the world's needs.
  —Frederick Buechner, American Author & Theologian

Purpose Statement Activity

In her book, *The Purposeful Hustle*[5], Deanna Singh, Founder and Chief Change Agent of Flying Elephant, asks readers to think how their experiences *uniquely position* them to make an impact.

The idea of what we are uniquely positioned to do resonates with me. You've probably heard of the Gallup's *CliftonStrengths*[6] assessment (or others like it), which has garnered international success by helping users identify their top talents for maximum leverage in the workplace.

If you are a strong communicator, for example, you are more likely to enjoy a career where you can regularly share your thoughts. You would probably be bored out of your mind working in isolation — which might be exactly what someone else needs to do their best.

To be clear, just because you are good at something doesn't mean that you should do it as a career. This is a theme that comes up over and over again when I coach PhD students and postdocs. Rather, I interpret Singh's quote as a call to action. How can you weave together your expertise and your purpose in a way that is satisfying to you and to potential employers?

Take for example some of my coaching clients who self-select out of potential jobs because they are *certain* that gaps in their skills, experiences, etc. disqualify them. Rather than taking a deficit approach, what if they started by naming what they care about and how they want to spend their time as the baseline for career decisions? This is where purpose statements can help.

TED speaker and mental health advocate, Dr. Julie Connor[7], says, "A personal purpose statement defines who you are and the mark you want to leave on this world. It provides clarity and reflects commitment to your goals. A purpose statement anchors you in the direction you want your story to go." Here are some example purpose statements:

> *I serve communities to promote collective wellbeing and center equity so that all people can live their most authentic lives.*
>
> *My purpose is to be compassionate and to support others as a friend, mentor, and colleague.*

You'll notice that the examples I've shared are really broad. That's because purpose statements reflect a vision for your *life*. Your purpose isn't limited to one career or situation. Jobs and activities change, but your purpose is nimble. It will move with you throughout your lifetime.

Below, take a few minutes to draft your purpose statement.

How did it feel to create your purpose statement? Coming from academia where precision is key, it's uncommon to frame ideas or processes in a way that seem like generalizations. Yet, creating high-level parameters is the first step toward focusing your career search.

If, for example, your purpose statement is about supporting children to grow and thrive, you'll probably feel unsatisfied if your career doesn't provide opportunities to promote the wellbeing of children. Tighten your search by focusing on jobs that fulfill aspects of supporting children to grow.

Next, think expansively about the different ways that you can support children to grow and thrive as a career. For instance, you could work with state government around youth childcare policies. You could lead a nonprofit that creates affordable housing for low-income children and families. Or you might develop educational apps that promote early literacy. The list goes on and on. What doesn't change is supporting children to grow and thrive.

In the process of centering your purpose, you might exclude potential job opportunities. That's the point. That's where the narrowing happens.

I can't overemphasize the power of separating what you are *trained to do* from what you *want to do*. Depending on how much your purpose has driven decision-making along your journey, what you *can do* and what you *want to do* may be very different things.

Where your talents and the world's needs cross, there lies your vocation.
—Aristotle

Advocate for Communities
Dadit Hidayat, Environmental Studies

As a policy and outreach specialist at a statewide nonprofit, Dadit was recruited for his expertise in community engagement. For the past decade, his research, teaching, and service initiatives have centered community-based solutions that demonstrate appreciation for local knowledge.

"Research is perceived as an elite industry mostly operated by people in higher-ed who tend to care more about documenting their work in academic journals, reports, and posters than on its impacts on community wellbeing.

Suppose PhDs have an awareness of their privilege. In that case, the degree can serve as a tool for elevating historically 'excluded' communities and advocating for their role as equal partners in research-relevant conversations. It can offer credentialed legitimacy to manage perceptions of research itself: a way to generate useful information that helps communities improve their lives.

Partnering with communities opens so many doors for learning. I'm not attached to a specific area. I care about what communities care about, from food justice to early childhood education. When PhDs separate their topical expertise from general research methodologies, the possibility of different jobs opens-up. You can get interested in almost anything."

TOP TIPS: PERSONAL BRAND

One of the first steps as you enter the job market is crafting your *personal brand*. Your personal brand is your public identity and reflects your values, talents, goals, and passions, and helps you communicate why you're a unique asset to an organization.

To communicate your personal brand, you'll want your content (writing, visuals, etc.) and medium (website, social media, print) to fit your image and reach the kind of employers you're looking to attract. You can go a traditional route using services like LinkedIn to create your professional profile.

Or consider joining a virtual community like Prof2Prof[8]; a free platform for academic professionals to connect, create public profiles that can serve as their professional landing pages, and share resources for teaching and research.* Putting together a simple website is another option, and many companies like Wix and GoDaddy offer services that help get your site live quickly and at low or no cost.

You can also create a simple logo to represent your brand. Include it in your email signature block, resumé, and reference materials. Why not make your own business cards? It's an inexpensive and simple way to convey professionalism when you're networking or interviewing. Websites like Fiverr and Upwork can connect you with low-cost freelance services to help with simple design work.

---

* Prof2Prof founder, Kristen Slack, has spent her career in academia in a variety of roles including full professor, PhD program director, department chair, etc. She is also an academic entrepreneur and higher ed innovator. You'll have a chance to read more about her journey later in the workbook.

Purpose Venn Diagram Activity

At the nexus of what you love to do, what you are great at, what the world needs, and what you can get paid for is your purpose. The concept is illustrated below by the *Purpose Venn Diagram,* which recently gained attention when Marc Winn adapted the model as the *Ikigai Venn Diagram*[9]. Ikigai is a Japanese concept that roughly translates to "one's reason for being."

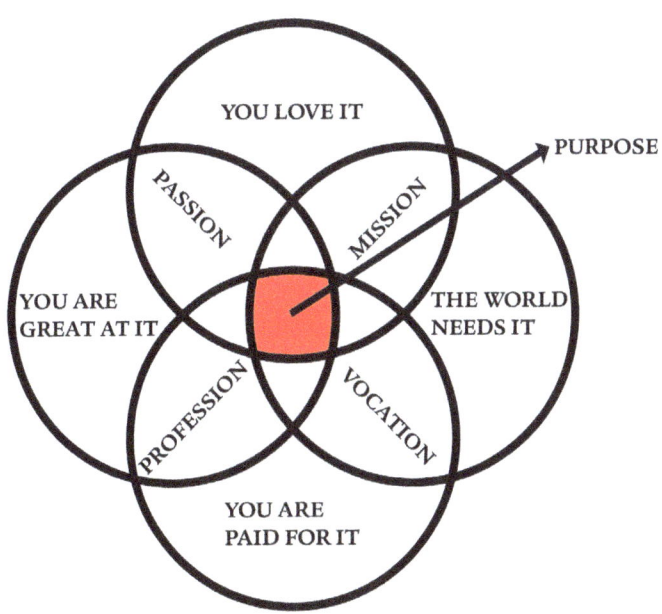

Doing what you love means doing things that energize and satisfy you. You might be someone who enjoys the arts and gravitates toward a job that inspires creativity.

Doing what you are great at is pretty clear-cut: Leverage your strengths. If math comes easily to you, for example, a career that works with numbers could be rewarding.

Doing what the world needs speaks to serving others. We feel fulfilled when we are helping out.

Finally, doing what you can get paid for helps separate hobbies from activities that provide an income. In other words, a career places a monetary value on what you do.

As you can imagine, it's hard to find a job that includes *everything* you love to do, are great at, what the world needs, and what you can get paid to do. It's helpful, however, to think about a few priorities in each area that can help you to evaluate potential jobs.

If a job looks like it will have a decent amount of overlap with what matters to you, that's a good starting place to consider whether it will be a match.

Below, take five minutes to list ideas that correspond with each section of the Purpose Venn Diagram. Feel free to include personal and professional activities and interests. Don't limit yourself to things you currently do — focus on the things that you aspire to do in your ideal world.

Note

I want to make a distinction between centering your purpose and the popular phrases, "Do what you love! or Follow your passion!" For one thing, many people don't have a singular passion. Although passion can result from doing things you love and excel at, it's not the only driver of career satisfaction. Answering the needs of an organization, community, or society are often part of the equation, as are income potential, work environment, etc. That's why 'purpose' — not passion — is at the center of the diagram.

Now think about how you realistically spend your time. Circle the items in your list that you do regularly. How many items did you circle compared to what you wrote? In other words, what is the difference between what you like to do and how you *actually* spend your time? What changes could you make so that your passion and mission align with your profession and vocation?

It doesn't interest me what you do for a living. I want to know what you ache for, and if you dare to dream of meeting your heart's longing.
—Oriah, Canadian Author

Take the Leap

Lauren Usher, Developmental Psychology

After finishing her PhD, Lauren was at a turning point. Should she pursue an academic job? If not, what would she do? Like many newly minted PhDs, she chose to do a postdoc to buy more time to make her decision.

Soon after accepting the position, she started exploring her next career move. For a few months, Lauren struggled with applying to the academic job market before pivoting her approach to jobs that maximize opportunities to interact with people and make a direct impact.

*She began her search online, **focusing on specific day-to-day tasks rather than a type of job or sector**. A key word for her search was "social interaction." To her surprise, one of the job listings that best aligned with her interests and values was as a director for a startup accelerator. The position was charged with running programs for entrepreneurs and others who want to make positive social change.*

At first glance, it seemed like the job was outside of her area of expertise. How could she make the case that she was qualified? After all, she had no previous business experience.

Lauren pitched her doctoral training as the ideal background for a job involving time management, multitasking, prioritizing, self-advocacy, researching quickly and in-depth, and communicating complex ideas to different audiences.

> *Lauren landed the job, left her postdoc, and hasn't looked back. Within a year of being hired, she was promoted to a management position, quickly proving her leadership capacity.*
>
> *If you're interested in a job in the startup space, Lauren suggests talking with a lot of different people to find out what they do from day-to-day. Get clear on what you want your job to look like: Busy days? High salary? Travel? Flexible schedule? High-achieving colleagues? Something else?*
>
> *"Someone recently told me that they view a PhD as a personal development pathway. I agree that it is one path to personal development, but I really think the 'why' behind the choice to embark on this path matters."*

Baking Cakes

Getting clear on your sense of purpose can be surprisingly difficult! This is especially true if you have been repeating a *should* narrative your whole life.

If you battle judgement about who you should be or what you should do, be gentle with yourself. Teasing apart social constructs, expectations from others, and your own inner critic from a deeper sense of knowing is hard work. There is often a lot of unlearning to do.

You might find that there is a disconnect between what you're good at — and can get paid for — and how you want to spend your time. Your work is to slow down the process of choosing a job and taking stock of what you're great at, what you enjoy, and what will have an impact you can stand behind.

Here's an example: I know a pastry chef with a thriving business. A year ago, he was churning out standard cakes by the dozen. Financially, he was set, but at a deep, personal level, making the same cakes over and over again wasn't satisfying. He was a gifted artist and wanted to work with a niche group of patrons interested in the artistry of pastry design.

Today, rather than being commissioned for hundreds of cakes each year, his goal is to create fifty. Each one will cost twenty times the generic versions — and take exponentially more time to prepare — but the results will be more than cakes. They will answer a call for art that captures a pivotal moment . . . and also be delicious!

What kind of cakes do you want to bake?

Your profession is not what brings home your weekly paycheck, your profession is what you're put here on earth to do, with such passion and such intensity that it becomes spiritual in calling.
—*Vincent van Gogh*

TIPS FOR YOUR STAGE OF THE JOURNEY

Pre-PhD: When you research PhD programs, look at their mission statements. Do they align with your purpose? Spend time reviewing faculty profiles. Are there particular professors who seem like they might be a good fit for your research interests and values? I encourage you to contact program administrators and faculty to ask questions about fit. It's a much less risky investment of your time — and theirs — to ask your questions before you apply for a program than waiting until you start and realizing that the fit is off.

PhD: How are you spending your time during grad school? Are you making space for the activities and relationships that are most important to you? Think of one thing that aligns with your purpose that you haven't done in a while. Can you do that thing for 15-minutes today? How can you honor your purpose, values, and interests as part of your grad school experience? Start practicing the lifestyle you want to embody — even in small ways — once you graduate.

Post-PhD: As you reflect on your Purpose Venn Diagram and Purpose Statement, what values, interests, and activities stand out? What are ways that you can incorporate a few of your priority areas into your job search? Could you review a job description with a different approach? For example, take note of key responsibilities that run parallel to what you want to do rather than checking to see that you have the skills required for the job.

SECTION 3

Shape Your Life Around Your Values

HOW DO YOU create personal goals that are meaningful and worthy to *you*? What beliefs motivate how you make decisions? What fundamental truths determine how you act?

According to a 2018 systematic review of values measures[10], psychologists, Kristin Serowik and colleagues, found that the ability to act in alignment with your values has a big effect on your life satisfaction and psychological wellbeing. Conversely, not living by your values is associated with increased rates of depression and anxiety. So what does this have to do with your career decisions? Basically, everything . . .

Your beliefs become your thoughts,
Your thoughts become your words,
Your words become your actions,
Your actions become your habits,
Your habits become your values,
Your values become your destiny.

—Mahatma Gandhi

Find Your Personal "Why"

Linda Vakunta, Environment & Resource

"I am a deputy mayor for the city of Madison, Wisconsin, with housing, health, and human services in my portfolio. All the jobs I've had dealt with people in very direct ways. That comes with pluses and challenges. I appreciate my training in qualitative research because measuring impact on people's lives and livelihood has significant qualitative components.

For any career, you have to find your personal "why." Why are you doing it? To what end? How will it help you in what you want to do next year, five years from now, twenty years from now?

More importantly, take time to know yourself. Who are you? What are your values? What do you like, dislike? Take care of yourself. Doing the inner work helps many aspects of your life, including your study. Personal wellbeing is important for doing the work."

Your values, like other aspects of your identity, might be invisible — *even to you*. At work, how you value your time, autonomy, and salary, for example, are areas where values can bump up against social norms and organizational policies without intentionality to the conditions. Whether or not you'll be expected to work after business hours or on weekends, or if a position requires 50% travel time, for example, may or may not conflict with your values and how you want to spend your time.

Values are proxies for aspects of lifestyle that matter most to you. Given the choice, what kind of lifestyle do you want?

When it comes to your job search, the goal is to find employers who nurture conditions to live your values — especially those most meaningful to your identity.

Organizational Culture

Unlike the tenure track in academia, organizations across sectors have myriad paths for promotion and vastly different policies that govern when and how it happens. In Frederic Laloux's seminal book *Reinventing Organizations*[11], he outlines conditions that contribute to cutting-edge practices gleaned from studying organizations around the world. Those conditions include a self-managing structure and an organizational culture characterized by a sense of wholeness and purpose.

In the book *Going Horizontal*[12], applied ethnographer, Samantha Slade, describes the future of organizational design. Per Slade, organizations that rely heavily on *horizontal structures* — a variation of self-management — minimize hierarchies, promote

---

Put YOURSELF First
Julia Gilden, Biomedical Science

"I am a senior scientist at a biotech company. Something your academic mentors won't tell you is to leave academia when it works for YOU, especially if you want to live somewhere with a smaller job market. There will never be a perfect moment to leave and spending another year writing one last paper won't matter nearly as much as snagging a great job when it's open. Put your career first and explore opportunities when they arise.

Sometimes in academia, we are taught that work should be the centerpiece of our lives. That can be really rewarding, but it can also be incredibly stressful. It can lead us to exclude things from our lives that bring us joy. I feel lucky to have a job that is interesting and challenging, but leaves time, space, and financial resources for other things that give me purpose, like family and service work. I lead a fuller, better, and more productive life than when I was engaged in academic science."

collaboration, creativity, respect, employee retention, productivity, and are often purpose driven.

How will I know if I'd like something like a horizontal organization?

For some people, the idea is intuitive: they like working in teams, are self-motivated, and enjoy the feeling of shared ownership for an organization's success. Other people feel confused by the whole idea. How will they explain their role to clients, or even to themselves? Who has the ultimate decision-making power in that kind of organization? How does promotion work? Uncertainties naturally arise when power structures are dismantled.

Consider the following questions: what if your supervisor is younger than you or has less formal education? What if the amount of time on the job plays no bearing on who is selected for the next big project, client, or promotion? How does that sit with you? Be honest with yourself before deciding if an organization's culture is a good fit.

> **Shape Your Direction**
>
> **Geoffrey Cureton, Applied Physics**
>
> *"Having a master's degree is sufficient for my job as academic staff at a large research university. My boss has a master's degree. But having a PhD gives me more control over the progression of my career, as I can participate more directly, and sooner, in the pursuit of research funding."*

One Piece of the Puzzle

You may have been socialized that going onto the job market means taking any tenure track opportunity that you're offered, no matter where it's located, nor the implications for your quality of life. If this has been your reality, taking a different approach to choosing a career can feel completely disorienting.

For many grad students and postdocs, career decisions orbit around the coveted tenure track professorship, often at the expense of other priorities. On the other hand, what if your purpose, values, and the impact you want to make on society guided your choices, rather than accommodating a single career outcome? The graphic below illustrates this idea.

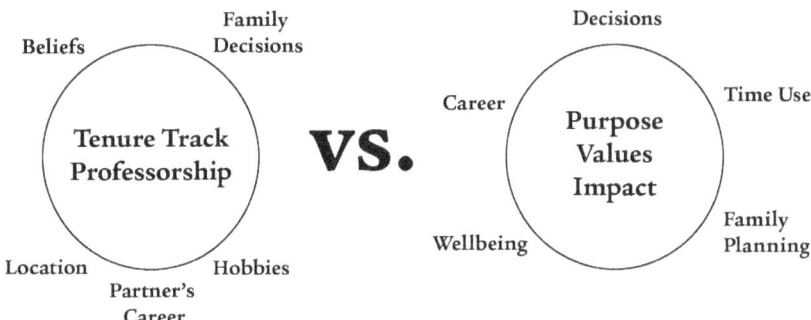

Make no mistake, part of what makes the tenure track so appealing is the lifestyle. The job boasts prestige, a flexible schedule, sabbaticals, and often, resources for conference travel and other perks. However, it's important to check-in with the reality of long hours, high expectations for publishing, grant writing, team management, student engagement, service, and acceptance that job security only comes after you receive tenure. As with every job, ask yourself, what are the benefits, and what are the costs?

Your career will be one — and only one — piece of your life. How do you want the whole puzzle to look?

When you plan for your career, think about what role you want your values to play in and out of the workplace, and be prepared to compromise. If you value being able to call your own shots, you might be willing to make concessions in other areas of the job, if an opportunity with significant autonomy arises. If you value living in the same town as your closest friends, or in a city that has affordable housing, these are factors you'll want to consider before accepting a job.

Keep in mind that the cultural standards across industries are constantly shifting. You'll find that some private sector jobs expect flexibility around relocation while others don't. Some government jobs will require that you live in the city or the county where you work. Most universities only hire faculty who received their doctoral training at a different institution. Some nonprofit jobs require no travel and others demand a lot. You'll want to ask hiring managers or other members of an organization what the expectations are instead of deferring to assumptions.

Ask Yourself, "What Motivates Me?"

Paul Creswell,
Population Health Sciences

"If you get a degree that qualifies you for work you don't enjoy, you aren't going to be happy or successful. So, ask yourself, what motivates you? Is it autonomy? Is it a specific topic? Is it lifestyle? Is it living in a specific place? Is it achievement? Is it relationships? Is it knowing things and understanding how they work?

For me, two fundamental values have guided me throughout my career. The first is environment (i.e., where I work/study) and the second is the personal connections I make in those environments. I once had a sticker that said, 'environment is everything.' I think that is accurate."

TOP TIPS: BUSINESS SAVVY FOR EVERY FIELD

Inside the walls of the academy, there is consensus that the pursuit of knowledge has value. Health disparities were a focus of my research in graduate school, and I'd grown accustomed to appreciation for the topic.

At my first private sector job in the population healthcare IT sector, I was horrified by the push-back when I suggested using our software to flag disparities across patient populations. No one praised the idea or shared my enthusiasm for the possibilities. Rather, the only question I was asked was to justify my *value proposition* — i.e., the business case — for why the idea mattered.

Naïve and accustomed to the presumed worth of my ideas within the academy, I was defensive. Who were these greedy idiots to suggest that there needs to be an economic case for addressing health disparities? Turns out, I was the idiot. Not for suggesting that health disparities matter, but for thinking that a decision in the private sector wouldn't consider the financial implications.

What felt like an affront to my values ended up being one of the most important lessons I learned in the private sector, and it has influenced the way I think in every job I've held since. No matter your personal beliefs or interests, if they don't align with what a consumer will buy or a funder will invest in, it's going to be hard to gain traction.

Save yourself from learning these lessons the hard way, and let me introduce a few concepts from the business world that will serve you well when you propose — or *pitch* — your ideas.

First, every proposal usually gets some critique of the value proposition. Be prepared to share the benefits of your idea and why you are uniquely qualified to bring the concept to life. Think of a value proposition as analogous to the infamous "so what?" in academia.

Without clarity around your central argument, your thesis — or value proposition — is hard to defend. PhDs are well-equipped to design convincing arguments — hello, dissertation! — just remember that the priorities of your audience may or may not align with your personal values.

To further increase your knowledgebase, here are a few concepts from business that will serve you well in *any* industry:

Accounting: Whether you manage grants at a nonprofit, develop budgets for a department of city government, or put together year-end financial reports for your investors, a basic understanding of accounting is a must. Start with gaining high-level proficiency with Excel. You might also need to learn QuickBooks, or a similar accounting software.

Development: Development is a term that refers to raising money. Development can include attracting donors, submitting grant proposals, hosting benefits, and running capital campaigns.

Management: In many leadership roles, you are responsible for supervising staff, developing departmental goals, communicating expectations, providing feedback, and evaluating results.

Marketing & Communication: These include myriad ways organizations promote their initiatives, products, and services via social media, community events, promotional products, etc.

Do yourself a favor, while you have access to university resources, audit a business 101 course, or connect with your local Small Business Development Center (SBDC)[13] for free or low-cost business classes. Learning to manage people, programs, and services doesn't just happen. They are skills that take training to master. Regardless of where you land, having a little business savvy will serve you well.

> *I was realizing that the next phase of my life would not simply unfold on its own, that my fancy degrees weren't going to automatically lead me to fulfilling work. Finding a career as opposed to a job wouldn't come from perusing the contact pages of an alumni directory; it required deeper thought and effort. I would need to hustle and learn.*
>
> —Michelle Obama, *Becoming*

Owning Your Values Activity

What are the conditions in your life that matter most to you? In her workbook, *Be Bold, Be Brave, Be You*[14], Kyira Wackett, public speaker, artist, and therapist, asks readers to consider a series of questions about their values:

- *What excites me?*

- *What would I do without any fear?*

- *What is the lifestyle I am seeking?*

- *What values would I release if I wasn't ashamed of what others would think?*

Take a few minutes to answer the questions above, focusing on your career. Here are some example responses:

- *What excites me about a job?* It excites me to work with international partners and collaborators.

  - *What job would I take if I didn't have any fear?* I would open a clothing store that features local designers and small batch producers.

  - *What do I need from a job to compliment the lifestyle I am seeking?* I need a job that recognizes — and holds space for — the multiple hats I wear. I am a professional, and I am a wife, mother, friend, and social justice advocate.

> *What values would I release if I wasn't ashamed of what others would think?* I would take *any* job — no matter the title or the degree requirements — that fulfill my sense of purpose.

Below, take a few minutes to reflect on the values that came up for you.

The trick here is that you need to be honest with yourself. Sounds easy enough, but it gets complicated when your values clash with what you think you are *supposed* to do for your career. This is particularly true if you've been told that the ideal career is one thing and what you really want to do — or how you define what it means to be a successful professional — is another.

Shape Your Life Around Your Values

Call for Change
Samira Salem,
Political Economy & Public Policy

As Vice President of Diversity, Equity, and Inclusion (DEI) for a national nonprofit trade association, Samira is poised for change. A political economist by training, she joined the organization as a senior policy analyst, bringing a deep commitment to issues of equity. Starting with small steps, for example, disaggregating data by race and ethnicity, it soon became clear that her dedication to DEI could be her full-time job.

"When I accepted the VP of DEI role, I had no doubt it was the right decision. I have a passion about DEI that comes from lived and professional experience. My parents were immigrants from two different continents and different faiths. I was weaned on the principles of DEI and social justice, and a commitment to community.

These ideas have forged my career path — from working on issues of poverty and injustice in emerging countries, to community development work in Wisconsin. Locally, I've focused on supporting nonprofits to advance racial equity and deepen DEI in their organizations and including my recent work, where I've led several of my organization's research and policy efforts in this regard.

My PhD has opened doors to interesting and meaningful work that otherwise would not have been an option. I've noticed that having the degree has meant that people listen and value my opinion. There is a certain level of credibility, reliability, and expertise that the degree signals, which in my experience, prospective employers and others value."

Owning your values — and working with others who appreciate you because of them (not despite them) — matters to your career satisfaction, and ultimately, your wellbeing. It's important to recognize that how you prioritize your values can change depending on your stage of life or other circumstances. For example, as a mother of young children, my goal is to work 30 hours a week. Maybe I'll feel differently when the kids are older, or maybe not! What's key is awareness of your values and how you tend to them in all aspects of your life.

What are the conditions that support *your* values?

My Island

I vividly remember a cold winter night one February, less than a year after I finished my PhD. It was dark and ugly outside — a pretty accurate reflection of how I felt about my professional future. When I graduated, I was pregnant with my first child and too exhausted to take on a full-blown job search. I knew I didn't want to pursue the tenure track, but I had no idea what else was possible. So, when I received an offer to extend my graduate research assistantship into a full-time job, I took it without too much thought.

Within a matter of months of taking the position, I was bored and miserable. I felt like my colleagues still saw me as a student, and I struggled to forge a professional identity. And that is how it came to pass that — unprompted by tools or by way of example — I sat down that dreary February night and started to describe my "island."

My island symbolized my ideal career — a professional life so idyllic that it conjured up images of tropical vacations and sunny beaches. Farfetched as it was, the activity was an unexpected catalyst for understanding what I wanted for my professional future. For the first time, I stopped focusing on particular jobs for PhDs and started listing activities I wanted to perform, workplace conditions, and other values that aligned with the professional I wanted to be.

Some of the things I listed were that I wanted to interact with people — not just data. I wanted to work for an organization — no matter the industry — that cared about social justice and the betterment of society. I enjoyed opportunities to mentor younger colleagues, and I valued organizations that prioritized employee wellbeing.

I wanted time to play with my baby — and not just at night when we were both tired and cranky. I realized that if it was financially possible for my family, I wanted to work part-time. What it really came down to was that I wanted a more spacious schedule and a less hurried lifestyle. I wanted to stop feeling like I was running a marathon every day of my life.

More than my other criteria, the desire to work part-time was hard to admit to myself. All that training so that I could stay home to make finger paintings and watch PBS Kids before naptime? Actually, yes. That's exactly what I wanted.

I believed – without yet knowing exactly how — that I could make meaningful contributions to society no matter how many hours a week I worked. I refused to consider anything other than a full-time career as "less than."

Using my island criteria, I unknowingly entered a purpose-driven search that changed my life forever. After leaving my first job out of grad school, I accepted a position as an account manager at a start-up healthcare IT company. Next, I was the director of social impact evaluation for a group of mission-driven nonprofits. Then I became a small business owner. From there I worked as an evaluator, facilitator, coach, and educator to organizations in the private, public, government, and academic sectors. Most recently, I co-founded a nonprofit organization dedicated to collective wellbeing for all. With each experience, I have gained a new language, insight, and understanding of values unique to organizations and to myself.

And to my delight, I later read an essay by organizational behavior expert, Margaret Wheatley, who described "islands of sanity"[15] as places where meaningful work is done — and where people thrive — despite the distractions of the world. It looks like I was on to something!

What does this mean for you? Simply put, your dissertation committee members probably won't tell you that *anything* you value "counts" as valid criteria for evaluating job fit. So, if you are struggling to own the truth of what you most want in a job — or are hearing voices of judgment and shame — know this: *You* get to decide what criteria shape your job search, no one else does. Not your family, not society, and not your advisor. That is your work to do, and it will impact every aspect of who you want to be and how you want to live your life.

Indulge Your Entrepreneurial Spirit
Sabrina Dumas, Nutritional Sciences

Sabrina's entrepreneurial spirit guided her path through grad school. Realizing she didn't want a career as a bench scientist, Sabrina prototyped a spin-off company from her dissertation research. The experience provided opportunities to meet with potential customers and become more knowledgeable about the start-up world.

Ultimately, Sabrina pursued a job as a clinical research liaison at a biotech company to begin her career. She is learning more about the private sector and using her PhD to brand herself as an expert in her field. Sabrina feels like the PhD credential will be an important asset as she works toward her dream job as a medical science liaison.

For other students interested in the private sector and start-up spaces, Sabrina recommends checking out free activities offered by many universities to get a better sense of the issues that the industry faces.

> *In a cemetery once, an old one in New England, I found a strangely soothing epitaph. The name of the deceased and her dates had been scoured away by wind and rain, but there was a carving of a tree with roots and branches (a classic nineteenth- century motif) and among them the words, "She attended well and faithfully to a few worthy things." At first, this seemed to me a little meager, a little stingy on the part of her survivors, but I wrote it down and have thought about it since and now I can't imagine a more proud or satisfying legacy. "She attended well and faithfully to a few worthy things."*
> —Reverend Victoria Safford, Unitarian Universalist Minister

The next set of activities will help you get clear on what your values look like in practice. In the meantime, here are some examples from PhDs and postdocs whom I've met:

- *I value working on lots of smaller projects rather than one big project — it's more stimulating.*

- *I like giving my full attention to one project before moving to the next one — it helps me focus.*

- *It's important to me that a job offers upward mobility — I want opportunities for growth.*

- *I want to be at an organization that offers remote working options — I have a health condition that makes in-person work challenging.*

What do your values look like to you?

Values Mapping Activity

In the last exercise, you clarified your values. In the following activity — the "Values Inventory"[16] — you'll explore how your values translate to different aspects of your career.

Below are several work-related values. Start by rating each from 1-4 using the following scale:

> 1 = Not Important at All 2 = Not Very Important
> 3 = Somewhat Important 4 = Very Important

Category I: Content of Work

___ My work is challenging.
___ My work involves high-level decision-making.
___ I have autonomy in my work; I set my own work priorities.
___ My work requires me to be a leader or a supervisor to others.
___ My work is detail oriented.
___ My work is intellectually stimulating.
___ My work requires a lot of creativity.
___ I am continually learning on the job.
___ My work contributes to others' wellbeing and helps others.
___ The are many deadlines and pressure.
___ My work has a lot of variety.
___ My work encourages self-expression.
___ My work involves risk.
___ My work includes adventure.
___ I have the same daily routine.

Category II: Benefits of My Work

___ I earn a large salary for my work.
___ People respect me for the work that I do.

___ There is room for advancement and promotion.
___ My organization acts with integrity.
___ I am perceived as influential or powerful because of my position.
___ My work gives back to the community.
___ People admire or look up to me for the work that I do.

Category III: My Work Environment

___ My workday is flexible, and I can set my own schedule.
___ It is quiet so I can focus on my work.
___ There is diversity among the people with whom I work.
___ I work indoors in a pleasant setting.
___ My work environment is fast paced.
___ I am safe in my work environment.
___ The pace where I work is relaxed.
___ I work with the public frequently; I interact with many people.
___ My workday is predictable.
___ I work outdoors.

Category IV: The People with Whom I Work

___ I work frequently with co-workers in teams.
___ I trust my co-workers.
___ My colleagues and I are very competitive.
___ There is harmony among my colleagues.
___ My co-workers care about me.
___ Humor is important to my colleagues and me.
___ My colleagues are very similar to me.
___ My co-workers are loyal.
___ My colleagues let me work on my own and do not interrupt me when I am working.
___ My colleagues appreciate individualism.
___ My colleagues differ from me, and I learn from our differences.

Next, select your top 10 values and describe how they connect with specific tasks. For example:

Value: My work gives back to the community.

Work-related tasks: I'll have support from leadership to share my work at public libraries, schools, and neighborhood centers so that community members can learn from our research.

How do your values connect with how you want to spend your time at work and what you want to do?

Shape Your Life Around Your Values

Live YOUR Way

Jennifer Skolaski,
Human Ecology: Community and Nonprofit Leadership

"Being a consultant allows me to work on a variety of issues that I am passionate about, like domestic abuse prevention, community safety, continuing education, substance use, poverty, transitional housing, youth leadership, and more.

The fact that I get to work on so many topics and always feel challenged makes me love my job even more. Every project is new and different, and I always get to learn the subject matter on the job. At this point I think I'd get too bored in a single organization or in a single role.

I also love the flexibility of my schedule. I'm able to spend more time with my kids. The negative is that I have to work some nights and weekends, and that I'm always "on." But it's an easy price to pay to know I can set my own schedule and be with my kids when they need me."

Your Values in Focus

It's surprisingly easy to overlook your values when you are evaluating potential jobs, especially if you're anxious to get your career started.

But how will I know if an organization aligns with my values?

The honest answer is that you won't know 100% until you start. That said, you can learn a lot about an organization before accepting a position. Check their website to see if they list their values, many do. Review their mission statements, goals, and priorities. How do they align with yours? What's missing? Talk to people who work there and/or have worked there in the past, or visit websites like Glassdoor, where current and former employees anonymously review companies.

Practice *values transparency* during interviews. That means sharing one or two top values-aligned criteria you look for in a job. These could be anything from the desire to work toward a leadership role, the opportunity to incorporate social justice into organizational planning, or the importance of having job security. If your main value clashes with the organization, the job might not be a good fit.

Your values also come into focus during negotiations. When I first graduated with my PhD, I valued financial security, so I negotiated hard on salary. During my next job search a few years later, I was burnt out from my previous role. So rather than prioritizing salary, I focused on getting my time back and negotiated for an 80% position that allowed for a more spacious lifestyle. Be creative about how your values influence all aspects of the job search.

Life Stage and Circumstances

The values that matter when you are looking for a job might change depending on your life stage and circumstances. It's okay to value a higher salary over other factors. It's okay to value stability over more dynamic options. It's okay to find satisfaction from working long hours with laser focus. It's okay to take a job that allows you to coast on autopilot during a stressful period of your life. None of these factors are mutually exclusive nor are they static. In other words, you can earn a healthy income *and* have a vibrant career. What's important to acknowledge is that what you want from a job can change over time.

Place Matters

I recently coached Erin who shared that after earning her PhD in psychology, she dreamed of working in a beautiful space. I was intrigued. After years of crunching numbers in a small basement office with no windows and florescent lighting, Erin hoped to work in a space that brought in nature — anything from pleasant views to abundant indoor plants. She valued the joy a beautiful esthetic inspires.

After graduating, Erin accepted a job as the director of youth programming for a nonprofit. The organization's mission is to improve childhood mental health through outdoor engagement. Her role offers ample opportunities to design outdoor initiatives, and she regularly visits clients and staff in the field. While she still works in an office building, the space is alive with pictures of kids enjoying the outdoors, and her organization's culture values nature. For Erin, the look and feel of the environment has made a huge difference in her wellbeing.

Decide What You Want

Allison Gold, Human Development and Family Studies

"I am a program associate at a nonprofit social research organization. I also have an LLC that offers project-based consulting and coaching. Research expertise is increasingly sought after in organizations that are not necessarily research focused. A PhD can help with getting a higher starting salary and the speed of your career growth. It really depends on the type of job you want and what you value."

TIPS FOR YOUR STAGE OF THE JOURNEY

Pre-PhD: Depending on where you are in life — finishing undergrad, a seasoned professional, or somewhere in-between — your lifestyle goals and values will be different. You might be thinking about whether it makes sense to take time off between undergraduate and graduate school or how a PhD fits in with your already busy career schedule. Regardless, ask yourself why you want to start a PhD in the first place. If you're unsure of the answer, take the time to clarify your goals and values before applying. A PhD adds value to any career but is not required for most.

PhD: In the middle of a PhD program, it can be hard to think about lifestyle goals when so much of your time and energy goes to just staying afloat. Reframing graduate school as part of your life — *rather than your whole life* — is critical to staying engaged, healthy, and strong for the long haul. The colleagues whom I've seen prioritize their values and lifestyle goals during grad school still ended up with the jobs that they wanted, and most importantly, their sanities intact.

Post-PhD: Even after you land a job, write down your values and keep them in a place where you can see them. If you've taken the time and effort to find a job that aligns with your lifestyle goals, honor them once the work begins. Remember that peer pressure is not just a kids' game! The start of a new job is a great time to set expectations for yourself and with your colleagues. If, for example, you return every email within five minutes of receiving it, you set a standard that others will come to expect. Likewise, if you return emails within 24 hours, colleagues will adapt to your pace.

SECTION 4

Make an Impact

HOW WILL YOU translate your expertise into ideas that matter? Where will your gifts and talents be put to good use? What approach will you use to leave your mark on society?

Your answers speak to your **impact**.

Impact is the effect or influence you have on people, places, and things. When I think about different ways to make an impact with a PhD, a major factor is the industry — or sector — where you work, e.g., private, nonprofit, government, or academia.

In addition to factors like location and income potential, something you might not have thought about is your **vehicle for impact**, or how you want to affect change.

You cannot get through a single day without having an impact on the world around you. What you do makes a difference, and you have to decide what kind of difference you want to make.
  —Jane Goodall, English Primatologist & Anthropologist

Vehicles for impact include policy reform, research-based initiatives, development campaigns, community outreach, models of leadership, and so on. The tools and strategies that bring your ideas to life are often tied to the sector where you work.

For example, the following are careers in various industries that address wellbeing in different ways: an advocacy job that influences how funding is steered toward community health initiatives (vehicle: public policy); a career in a private sector biotech company that develops tools and products to promote wellbeing (vehicle: technology); a career in the nonprofit sector that engages community members to create local wellbeing indicators (vehicle: community engagement), or a career in academia where you can share your latest health research findings with a global audience of scholars and practitioners (vehicle: publication).

In sum, different industries excel in varying ways that impact their clients, customers, and society. Taking stock of how you want to address the issues you care about — whether that is a specific disease state, automation process, gene mutation, or policy issue — matters when you think about your career. Also true is that the pace of change may be faster or slower depending on the organization or sector. Whereas a slower, more meticulous pace and process is a hallmark of academia, rapid failure and refocusing is common in the start-up world.

> *But I'm not qualified for a career in the private sector (or fill in the blank)! Won't I need another degree?*

These are some of the concerns that I hear the most. I want to answer them in two parts:

I'm Not qualified! Am I?

A postdoc recently told me that she was only eligible for entry-level jobs in the private sector. After reading several position descriptions, she concluded that more senior positions required management experience, which she didn't have.

EXAMPLE CAREERS IN ACADEMIA

Tenure Track Professor	*Curriculum Developer*
Clinical Faculty	*Researcher*
Adjunct Faculty	*Grants Manager*
Program Administrator/Director	*Outreach Specialist*
Advisor	*Continuing Education Manager*

Hearing this, I asked if she had ever helped to hire and/or supervise undergraduate or master's students in her lab. She had. I asked her if she had ever been the project coordinator for a study? She had. I asked if she had ever been asked to provide feedback to her colleagues after a big presentation. She had.

Given these aspects of her position, we talked about how, in fact, she had management experience. Later in this section, I'll talk about transferable skills and provide examples of how to repackage your training in ways that resonate with employers across sectors.

More School? Unlikely.

It's rarely the case that I meet a PhD who needs another degree to land a job. For some specialized jobs, certifications are required — or make your application more attractive — like a project management credential, for example. But that credential is often a short course and by no means another degree.

More important than another degree is whether you understand what a company or industry values. If you're looking for a job in the private sector, start by taking a free massive open online course (MOOC) from some of the world's top universities to get familiar with industry lingo. Make it obvious to employers that you're up-to-speed on the things they care about.

Bottom Line: Don't self-select out of a job because you assume you don't qualify!

The Thrill of Innovation
Kristen Slack, Social Welfare

"My career is in transition. I am a full professor at a large, public university, where I have worked for 20 years. I am also an ed-tech entrepreneur who developed a business stemming from my journey within academia, and my observations on how that space could be improved.

I would have never guessed, early on, that I would have the skills required to create an ed-tech company from the ground up. However, it turns out that years of applying analytical skills in the pursuit of answering research questions, designing courses, speaking to large audiences, facilitating discussions, running academic programs, mentoring students, and taking on administrative leadership roles couldn't have prepared me much better.

It's thrilling to be doing something that feels totally new, but also completely natural, given the career trajectory that I've had."

Crafting Your Pitch

I was recently chatting with a friend who was *thrilled* that her daughter, Sage, had landed a well-paying job at a major manufacturing company. The job came as a surprise because Sage had a background in gender studies and the job focused on data visualization.

Using her experience as a volunteer data analyst for local start-ups, Sage strategically crafted her application to play up her hobby to a

EXAMPLE CAREERS IN GOVERNMENT

Scientist	*Legislator*
Policy Analyst	*Administrator*
Program Officer	*Evaluator*

potential employer. She made the case, despite the fact that her degree was in a completely different field. Today, Sage is a *twenty-one-year-old* recent college grad who will soon be starting a job with a $75K salary plus annual bonuses.

PhD graduates and postdocs, take heed: Don't let years engrossed in academic culture fool you into believing that you can't take a job unless you are a bona fide "expert." Recent college grads are pitching their skills in creative ways — you can too, and so much more. You've got this.

Do not ignore a little spark; it can start a wildfire.
—Debasish Mridha, American Physician, Philosopher, & Author

Zooming Out

A quick way to increase your job prospects is to zoom out on your areas of expertise. For example, you may be part of a small group of scholars who study how a particular treatment affects African American teen boys suffering from severe depression. However, you are also a scientist who undoubtedly knows a considerable amount about the larger fields of youth mental health, cultural considerations in youth mental health treatment, and youth development. These broader areas of expertise position you for countless careers.

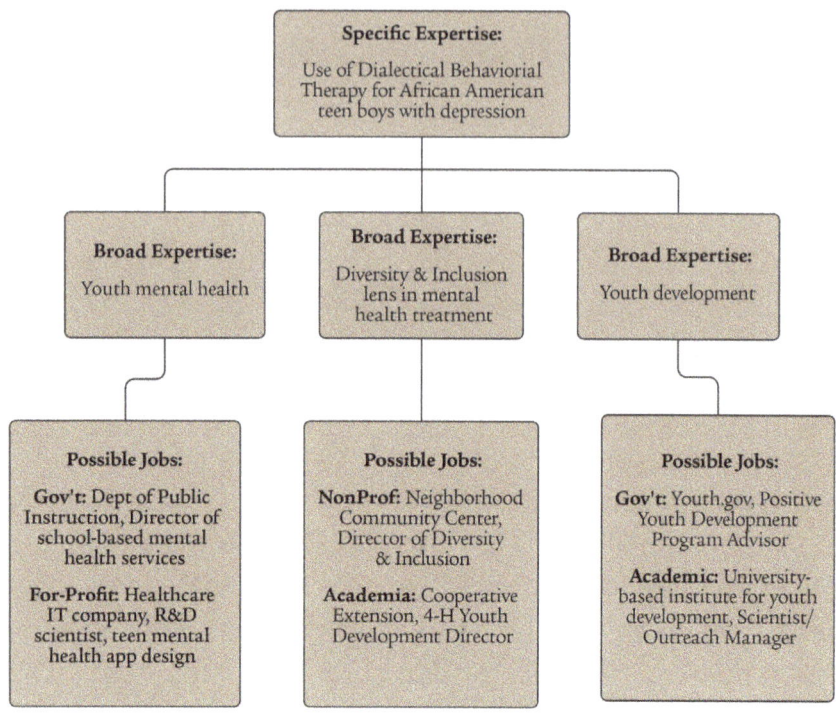

Say, for example, you're halfway through your postdoc and realize that while you love many of the activities that your job entails — interviewing research participants, analyzing complex models, and communicating results — you can't see studying the same topic for the rest of your career. This is where zooming out — combined with your PhD Superpowers — comes into play.

With all of your highly sought-after research, critical thinking, and management skills, you could broaden your options to land a career at just about *any* kind of company. You could make the case, for example, that your PhD in environmental engineering, combined with your passion for cars, make you the ideal project manager for a green automobile manufacturing company. With your clear communication skills, attention to detail, and love of the industry, it wouldn't be hard to make a case for why you are ideally suited for the job.

Interestingly, when I present the concept of zooming out, PhD students and postdocs sometimes tell me that it raises red flags. For example, as one woman put it, "I think I'm scared to zoom out because it seems like a big risk — how do I know it'll work out? If I look for jobs other than faculty, will I be closing that door as an option? It sort of feels like I'm '**giving up**' after coming so far... lots of anxiety of the unknown." Another client shared similar fears, "I feel like by zooming out, **you lose your concrete qualifications** from your specialization. That can make you feel unqualified for what's next."

These are real and valid concerns, and they underscore the very reason I wrote this book. Somewhere in graduate school, the belief is seeded that if you pursue any job other than the tenure track, you are "giving up," "losing out," or in short, *failing*.

This is a myth that needs to be put to rest. The belief that the tenure track has greater value than any other career is a dated social construction. Depending on your advisor or committee members, you may hear many different opinions on the topic. It will

Showcase Your Versatility
Pablo Parraga, Mechanical Engineering

"I've used my degree in government, industry, and academia in the United States, Sweden and Colombia. I feel like I have a profound knowledge of how things work. In every job, I don't always know what I'm going to do for the day, but I am always able to figure it out relatively quickly.

In my opinion, sometimes colleagues don't think too highly of PhDs. You don't need to hide it, but it does not have the same value outside of academia. Instead, focus on transferable skills and showcasing your versatility."

be incumbent upon you to honor your self-worth and to challenge this notion of failure that's been delivered to graduate students for decades. Only you get to decide what amounts to a successful career for you.

Career Ideation Activity

When I give talks, one of the first things I hear from graduate students and postdocs is,

> "So, what *are* these phantom non-tenure-track jobs you keep talking about?"

That's a great question. It can be hard to imagine how a PhD could lead to a career beyond the tenure track when so much of your training is shaped by faculty who've taken this path. The simple truth is that *any* job is possible with a PhD.

In the next exercise, I want you to brainstorm possible careers in different industries that are related to your broad field of study. Let's start by looking at examples for a PhD in Education:

- **Academia**: Instructor, Dean, curriculum advisor
- **Nonprofit**: Educational programming director, advocacy coordinator
- **Government**: Educational policy analyst, school board chair
- **For-Profit**: Research & development scientist for educational products, professional development consultant

Here's another set of examples for Biomedical Engineering:

- **Academia**: Researcher, advisor, grants manager
- **Nonprofit**: Licensing manager, director of research
- **Government**: Field engineer, sustainability director
- **For-Profit**: Drug designer, software engineer, medical scientist

EXAMPLE CAREERS IN THE PRIVATE SECTOR

Business Executive

Personal or Organizational Coach

Professional Development Trainer

Project Manager

Business Consultant

Data Scientist

Systems Change Manager

Now you try. Start by thinking about possible careers that leverage your unique interests. If you come up blank, Google your field and different job sectors. For example, "engineering" + "government jobs" or "mathematics" + "private sector jobs."

You'll be surprised at how many jobs will pop-up. Some hits will be actual job listings, and others will share example careers that someone with your degree might have. Obviously, not all of them will be a good match, but the results will shed light on careers you've never thought of — or even knew existed!

Note that I didn't include "PhD" in the search criteria. You will drastically limit your job options — and the boundaries of your creativity — by only looking for jobs that require a PhD. Many don't.

Academia:

The Purposeful PhD

Nonprofit:

Government:

For-Profit:

> ### Why Industry?
> ### Julia Gilden, Biomedical Science
>
> *"When you're interviewing for your first job outside of academia, you will ALWAYS be asked why you want to transition to industry. You need to make a strong case for what appeals to you about industry and demonstrate that you understand how the two sectors are different.*
>
> *Figure out how to talk about the work you've done that makes it applicable to industrial science. None of my work as a student or postdoc was remotely clinical, but by researching the company I wanted to work for and the kinds of products they develop, I was able to tell a story about how my skills would apply and what experience I had that would help me understand their products and customers."*

Don't be Afraid to Change Course

Chris Schacherer,
Psychology - Human Factors & Ergonomics

Throughout grad school, Chris worked at a big medical center as a statistical analyst, programmer, and research assistant. By the time he finished his degree, Chris realized that he liked his side gig in clinical research more than his studies.

Following his instincts, Chris continued working in clinical research as a software application developer and statistical analyst. Eventually he made the jump into the "business side" of healthcare by working on clinical quality measurement, provider reimbursement, and drivers of healthcare spending. One thing led to another, and soon Chris was working at some of the most prominent healthcare organizations in the country, helping people understand their data and the stories it could tell.

His vast experience in different areas of healthcare helped Chris develop a strong foundation to launch his own healthcare analytics consulting firm, which he leads today.

"It's thrilling to be doing something that feels totally new, but also completely natural, given the career trajectory that I've had."

TOP TIPS: TALKING THE TALK

You may be the most brilliant physicist, anthropologist, or political scientist, but if you can't communicate in a way that makes sense to other people, you'll miss out on job opportunities.

Outside of academia, you'll work with attorneys, project managers, finance specialists, marketing and development directors, consultants, and dozens of other professionals. Each of them will have their own talents, and potentially, none of them will overlap with yours.

Most of the workbook has been about identifying *your* purpose, *your* values, and *your* impact. This is exceptionally important work. But to land a job, **you'll need to make the case that what you can offer is what a company needs in a way that makes sense to them.**

It's easy to defer to talking about your research in an academic way. For any number of university-based positions, that lingo will serve you well. However, if you stand in front of many potential employers and start talking theory, modeling, or the particulars of your dissertation, you'll lose them before you begin. Don't be that PhD who needs to describe the minutiae of her research while other's eyes glaze over. Translate your expertise into their language, not the other way around.

One of the hardest things I have found working across sectors is that people have preconceived ideas of what it means to hire a PhD.

Surely someone with a PhD wears a white coat and dissects mice. Surely, they are awkward and nerdy and live with their heads in the clouds.

Right out of the gate, show employers that in fact, PhDs are eloquent and clear communicators, innovative thinkers, and team players. To do this, prepare to *talk the talk*. In other words, do your homework about what an organization cares about, and practice sharing what you do in a way they recognize and value. To prepare, start by spending time on their websites and social media pages, and by having informational interviews with professionals in the field. Not only will this help to build your network, but it will also enhance your industry-specific vocabulary.

The Hook

You'll need to make a connection — the "hook" — between the experiences you had during your grad and postdoctoral training and how they add value to other industries. These are referred to as transferable skills. Here are some examples:

PhD task or activity	Transferable Skills/competency
I wrote a 50,000-word dissertation.	Present & organize large amounts of information clearly.
My committee didn't get along.	Negotiation skills.
I analyzed tons of data.	Analysis of complex data.
I published papers, book chapters and presented at conferences.	Ability to communicate complex ideas in many formats.
I completed a PhD.	Work with minimum supervision and/or in teams.
I organized a conference.	Event planning experience.
My research group was international, or I spent some time abroad for my research.	Interact with colleagues from diverse backgrounds towards common goals.
Experiments failed; I kept trying until I found something that worked.	Perseverance, diligence, troubleshooting, problem-solving.
I balanced coursework, teaching, research, and home life.	Time-management, multitasking, supervision, mentorship.
I worked with colleagues to accomplish a research goal.	Teamwork, collaboration.
I needed a tool that was too expensive, so I prototyped a widget that worked just as well.	Creativity, cleverness, resourcefulness.
A colleague did something unethical, and I handled the situation in a professional way.	People skills, ethics, communication, professionalism.

Adapted from Mather-L'Huillier[17]

A CV or resumé isn't always the best place to showcase your transferable skills. That means that when you interview, you'll need to make it clear to employers that your unique talents set you apart from other candidates and are exactly what the organization needs to thrive.

Clear Communication Activity

This exercise is great for practicing straightforward, jargon-free communication. Talk with someone outside of your field, and explain your research in a practical and engaging way. If your listener looks bored or asks tons of clarifying questions, keep practicing. It's not hard to tell when you've lost someone's attention.

- How did the activity go?

- What was the hardest part? What was the easiest?

- Did you learn something that you didn't expect?

Once you have worked out how to explain what you do and why it matters, write it down here. It's always helpful to look back at your ideas before an interview.

_____

_____

_____

_____

_____

Let's take the exercise a step further. It's one thing to talk about your research clearly. It's another to present your ideas in a way that resonates with the industry where you want to work.

I'll use my research around health disparities as an example. Below you'll see how I take the same topic and adjust the messaging to reflect specific industry values and lingo:

Academia: I research social determinants of health and the disproportionate burden of disease experienced by low-income racial and ethnic communities.

Nonprofit: I care about the way a person's environment affects their health, especially in communities that lack basic resources.

Government: I analyze the ways social policies affect the health of marginalized communities.

For-Profit: I cut costs by identifying patients who use the emergency room for basic care rather than outpatient settings.

Now think about your research. Find a few job listings and review the

Tips from the Field
Yonah Drazen, Social Welfare

To prepare for jobs in state government and an academic research institute, Yonah credits his experiences working with state agencies and other non-academic stakeholders. Building relationships with a variety of individuals and agencies while he was in grad school helped him learn the kinds of products, values, and language that would resonate with future colleagues in the field.

"Networking is key. Working on a variety of different projects is also helpful as most firms require many different social science skills to carry forward their goals."

company mission statements and values. Next, write a brief description of your work in a way that demonstrates that you can meet their needs using language that reflects your industry knowhow.

Academia:

Nonprofit:

Government:

For-Profit:

EXAMPLE CAREERS IN THE NONPROFIT SECTOR

Agency Administrator	Development Director
Advocacy Organizational Leader	Grant Writer
Community Development Leader	Philanthropy/Foundation Leader
International NGO Leader	Think-Tank Researcher
Program Officer/Director	Professional Association Leader

Just like you prepare a unique cover letter for each job application, how you talk about your credentials may be very job specific. In fact, you might not end up talking about your research at all! Depending on the job, or the stage of your career, the research you did in grad school might not come up. Other experiences may be more relevant to the story you'll craft.

For example, if I were responding to a consulting opportunity to assess the impact of a civic engagement club for inner-city seniors, talking about my graduate school research working with young families caring for children with autism might not give the impression that I was qualified.

If instead, I outlined my extensive experience as a community-based program evaluator, as well as my understanding of factors that influence urban living, I would be more likely to demonstrate how and why I was right for the job.

In an age of speed, I began to think nothing could be more exhilarating than going slow. In an age of distraction, nothing can feel more luxurious than paying attention. And in an age of constant movement, nothing is more urgent than sitting still.

—Pico Iyer, British Author

Ask the Right Questions
Sisi Li,
Neuroscience Training Program - Psychiatry

"Being proactive and solving problems creatively has bolstered my success as a research scientist at a biotech startup. In grad school, I learned to organize my projects and figure out how to make things happen — anything from where to find the best information to knowing when and who to ask for help. Learning to ask the right questions is so important. I learned to be resourceful and to achieve success even when the initial results weren't great."

Find Support

Figuring out how to make an impact with your PhD is a matter of creativity. Your hook should inspire an employer to say, "I can *totally* see how someone with a PhD in English is a great fit as an administrator at the Business Development Center" or "Gee, I never thought someone with a PhD in Botany would be the top pick for our new development director, but it works!"

The key is how you package your skills and expertise so it's clear you are the ideal candidate for virtually any job you choose.

I'm still not sure I know how to do that...

You've heard from PhDs in a variety of careers throughout this workbook, but nothing can substitute for the power of a personal connection. Talking with someone who has a PhD and the kind of job you want — or even works in the same field — is invaluable when it comes to practicing your pitch. Ultimately, your advisor or principal investigator might not be able to provide the support you need. At every stage of your PhD journey (and beyond), seek out mentors that can help you grow.

But I don't know where to find those people!

When I do presentations, I like to remind audiences of the simplest "research" tool at their disposal: The almighty internet. Is there someone who graduated with your degree in a field that interests you? Google it. Also, check out thought leaders in your field on Twitter, and start to interact with their posts. Seriously. They might respond and start a conversation. You'll be surprised how quickly you can connect with people who share your interests.

If you're nervous about contacting someone new, be assured that often, people are flattered that you took the time to find them and would be happy to chat. And because you can talk with people anywhere by phone or videoconferencing, the possible career connections and mentor opportunities are nearly unlimited.

Another idea is to contact your field's professional organization; many have member service coordinators who can connect you with individuals who have volunteered to be mentors. This was the first networking strategy that I used to find a mentor with my credentials who was working in the kind of job I could envision for myself.

You can also reach out to your university or departmental alumni coordinator to connect with PhD graduates who pursued careers that appeal to you. People who share a university affiliation have an instant connection that makes for an easy icebreaker.

The Power of Networking
Sarah Lewis, Genetics

"I'm a postdoc seeking a job in industry. If you're a PhD student and don't know what you want to do, start early in exploration and informational interviews. Most people, especially those with "non-traditional" careers, are willing to talk briefly with you on the phone or in-person. Grow and utilize your LinkedIn network. IT WORKS. Join associations, clubs, and organizations on campus, or in the community that are related to what you want to do."

Keep in mind that the purpose of these connections is to listen to the other person, and potentially, to ask for feedback on how to present your ideas. While a secondary goal may be to plant the seeds for future employment, the main intention is to learn.

Out of the Box

At a large research university, I hosted a panel of PhDs working across industries. They had degrees in different fields, all had decided to pursue careers outside of academia, all had jobs they never could have pictured for themselves during grad school, and NONE of them had prior experience in the industry where they landed. An environmental scientist in government? An engineer in the nonprofit world? A psychologist in business? How did this happen?!

In each case, the speakers said the same thing: Take the time to know yourself and what you want to do professionally. Reach out to people who have the kinds of jobs you want. Then make it clear to an employer why someone with your background is the right fit for the job.

The Expert Myth
Paul Creswell, Population Health Sciences

"I am a researcher for a health institute at a large research university. Prior to that, I was a senior epidemiologist for a state environmental public health tracking program. Particularly in academia, there's a lot of expectation that you will become an "expert" in a specific area.

It's a myth that to become an expert you have to start by being passionate about only one topic. If you are open to being excited about a lot of different areas, you will always find interesting work. There's no shortage of important things to pursue."

TIPS FOR YOUR STAGE OF THE JOURNEY

Pre-PhD: You are in an ideal position to learn about and test out career options. One of the easiest ways to do that is by having informational interviews or shadowing professionals in industries where you could imagine working. You don't have to know exactly "what you want to be when you grow up" before applying for grad school. But if you know ahead of time that you are interested in careers outside of academia, you can start looking for mentors — including faculty — even before you apply for the degree. Mentors can share tips for ways to design your graduate school experience to prepare for specific jobs — including what courses to take, or what work or internship experiences will position you for success.

PhD: Talk with your advisor about who can be on your committee. Some programs allow a member from outside of the university who has relevant professional experience on your topic. Having someone on the team who understands the impact you want to make can be a powerful asset.

Contact your university's office of professional or career development. Many are starting to realize that students need more support to prepare for non-tenure-track jobs and offer presentations, seminars, and other resources.

At any stage in the game, connect with mentors in the industry where you want to work. They'll offer suggestions about how to use your time in grad school to prepare for your career.

Post-PhD: Connect with your university's Office of Postdoctoral Studies. Many have career resources for transitioning from academia to other industries. Continue to cultivate professional relationships by networking and seeking mentorship.

Know that there will be unlearning to do. By this point in your career, you may have been working on your PhD and postdoc for over a decade. That's a lot of time to be steeped in academic culture and values. While the academy can be extremely prescriptive, it is so important that you own your decision to choose a career that matters to you. You might never have your PI's support, and that's a tough pill to swallow. Like most things, though, you'll have a much bigger battle to fight if you choose a career out of obligation, guilt, or fear.

SECTION 5

A New Way Forward

NOW IS WHEN I start to get a funny feeling. It sneaks up on me at the end of every presentation — and, not surprisingly — as I near the end of this workbook. It's the fear that I've been disingenuous. That somehow, I've failed to address the biggest elephant in the room.

I ask myself if the subtext of this workbook is actually: *Just* make it through the archaic and constrictive model of today's PhD education and postdoctoral training, and be as intentional as you can within a deeply flawed culture of learning. But don't worry! On the other side, you will be happy and find a career that matters to you.

Who I really am keeps surprising me.
　　　—Nikki Giovanni, American Writer, Activist, & Educator

Something Seems Amiss...

For so long, the ethos of doctoral training has undermined the road to personal transformation and wellbeing. It has carved a career path so narrow that students and postdocs can feel disheartened, socially and intellectually isolated, and prone to self-sacrifice above self-discovery. This is especially true if their career aspirations veer outside the tenure track.

In their 2013 critique of doctoral education[18], Maximiliaan Schillebeeckx and colleagues share fascinating — and at times, disheartening — insights into the struggles of PhD students. Even more compelling is that they published their commentary *while still in grad school*:

> As graduate students, we have become disillusioned with our academic training. We began graduate school full of ambition, drive and optimism but have long since come to realize that we have joined a system that does not meet our diverse interests. We yearn for a community that supports creativity and the expression of future career goals instead of one with a narrow, focused interest.

For years, the research community has incentivized training opportunities that prepare graduate students for a host of career options. Yet, in an environment where the tenure track reigns supreme, top-down approaches have failed to change what is valued within the academy.

In her 2018 study[19], education scholar Dr. Isabelle Skakni suggests that "aspects of the academic world and culture — perpetuated, deliberately or not, by the scholarly community — likely impede students' progress."

Progress that I would argue is both academic and personal. The values of graduate training have largely negated the merits of self-reflection and career ideation by continuing to reward the tenure track above all others. Why would anyone do the deep, time-intensive work of exploring other options if there was no incentive or resources to do so?

As a result, I see PhD students and postdocs grieving the loss of an identity — and perhaps, an assumed sense of purpose — if the tenure track job doesn't pan out.

Be Aware of Your Motivation
Stephan Hiroshi Gilchrist, Educational Leadership

"I recently co-founded a nonprofit focused on collective wellbeing where I serve as Co-Director. Prior to that I was the director of a social innovation leadership graduate program at a small liberal arts college. There, I would tell students that I would not recommend pursuing a career as faculty unless they have a deep drive that is connected to their life's purpose.

Jobs are limited. Colleges and universities are looking to hire more and more adjuncts who get paid poorly and receive little or no benefits. You need to be very flexible about where you live. Higher education is changing, and the traditional ways we have thought about undergraduate and graduate education are not as relevant to the needs of communities.

So, ask yourself, are there different ways you can do what you'd like that are outside of higher education that may complement the work that is happening there? For example, teaching, researching, or being an administrator in a government, non-profit, or for-profit context that may even partner with a college or university? Focus on connecting to your true purpose (your intrinsic motivation), and don't pursue a position because of its social status or what others expect of you (external motivation)."

Personal Growth?

Graduate school is many things, but rarely do I hear it described as an opening for professional *and* personal growth. Grad school and postdoctoral training provide time and resources to master skills, gain experiences, and publish research. But have you ever stopped and asked yourself what it would be like if graduate school culture supported your highest potential, personally and professionally?

But is personal growth really the purpose of graduate school?

Perhaps personal growth is not *the* primary goal of getting a PhD or postdoc, but shouldn't it be one of them? Aren't they connected? If you're not encouraged to ask such fundamental questions as what you *really* care about and how you want to spend your time while you're in training, then when? Maybe this is why so many postdocs tell me they took the position because, frankly, they didn't know what else to do. They hadn't had time or support to consider other options.

So, I ask: When will deep personal exploration be a priority of graduate training? Is academe really doing a service to society by skirting the opportunity?

Take this example: I was recently chatting with a postdoc career counselor at an R1 university. Amidst the Coronavirus pandemic, one of his advisees — an *expert in lung infections* and the recipient of a coveted National Institutes of Health K award — came to him in distress wondering where her career was headed with the dearth of tenure track positions.

I had to stop and ask my colleague if he was joking. Surely this intelligent and experienced woman knew how desperately the world needed her — and thousands more like her — to help us get a handle on one of the biggest global health crises of our generation?

Surely she could see how her work had a place in every imaginable industry: leading research and development of vaccines and treatments at bio-tech companies, informing health policies in all levels of government, developing public awareness campaigns for nonprofits, and on and on.

Heartbreakingly, none of these possibilities were on her radar. At first, I gasped, then I laughed, and then I was devastated. How was it possible that a person with so much talent could have so little insight into her personal and professional worth? But who could blame her? The academy continues to neglect opportunities for students to see their value in jobs beyond the tenure track.

Fortunately, my colleague — a master reframer — asked his advisee to imagine her fears as opportunities. Rather than seeing the pandemic as a cause for fewer faculty positions, what if instead, they brainstormed dozens of career opportunities that have arisen in its wake?

It bears reminding, dear reader, that you are worthy and brilliant and needed — no matter what career you choose or what path you take to get there. *You* **are uniquely qualified to change the world with the strengths and experiences you bring to the table.**

The Silver Lining

I'm being *very* hard on the culture of graduate education. I know I am. I think about my own PhD advisor — now a cherished friend and confidant — who like so many, is doing the best she can. Amidst the backdrop of constant threats of budget cuts, unwavering regulations, and political turmoil, she offers students her compassion, mentorship, and time. Honestly, what more can she do?

Behold the Emerging Future

Jayne Bryant, PhD Student, Strategic Leadership towards Sustainability

In 2019, I attended an international gathering of researchers in Berlin, where I happened upon something that threw me for a loop: I met a doctoral student — Jayne, an Australian native studying in Sweden — who seemed pretty darn happy.

When Jayne talked about grad school, she shared plans to spend time in the United States, connecting with leaders in her field and hopes to collaborate with other teams in Europe and beyond. There was funding available for her travel and studies. Her ideas were supported by her advisor, and she had opportunities to share her experiences and burgeoning expertise with master's students whom she adored.

My jaw dropped. This wasn't a scenario I'd seen before. Here was a confident, empowered, delightful woman who gave me the impression that graduate school had actually facilitated her journey to becoming a better version of herself.

Jayne's experience could be for a number of reasons, of course, including how PhD students in Sweden are hired as staff similar to assistant professors in the States and provided with ample funding, or perhaps it had more to do with her disposition. Still, her story intrigued me.

Creating the Conditions

> *We live in an age of profound disruption where something is ending and dying, and something else is wanting to be born.*
> —*Otto Scharmer, Co-Founder of the The Presencing Institute*

On a whim, I took to social media asking friends and colleagues if they — or someone they knew — felt like graduate school helped to nurture the best version of themselves.

Within minutes I had a response, *"If you ever need stories about how grad school slowly eroded someone's self-worth, please just let me know!"* Then another and another, all in the same vein.

There were a few positive comments — mostly to do with setting good school-work-life boundaries and a nod to supportive advisers — but the majority were downers. And yet, I fail to believe that Jayne is the *only* person who feels like grad school helped foster her highest self.

So, I started questioning, what conditions lead to positive experiences in grad school and postdoctoral studies? What would it take for students to feel confident, supported, and empowered? What effect would this kind of encouragement have on the mental health of grad students and postdocs? Ultimately, what would it mean for a society to be flooded with talented and confident researchers poised to enhance every aspect of the planet?

I'm not the only person asking these questions. In their 2019 study of determinants of PhD student satisfaction[20], Gerard Dericks and colleagues build on an extensive literature exploring how factors such as the role of supervisors, departments, and peer qualities influence students' satisfaction with their doctoral programs.

With data from PhD students at 63 universities in 20 countries, they found that non-academic aspects of their supervisors' roles — what they characterize as "supportiveness" — are the most powerful predictors of student satisfaction, and shockingly, that supervisors' scholarly expertise — or "academic qualities" — have no effect.

The authors acknowledge that supervisor supportiveness can mean different things to different people. Perhaps, it means that an advisee feels confident to explore different career options without fear, shame, or guilt. Or maybe it means having access to a variety of career development resources and counseling. Or it could mean something completely different. We really don't know until we ask the question.

What I can assume after talking with hundreds of PhD students and postdocs, however, is that when they feel their work has merit, and that they have meaningful career option, collective wellbeing stands to improve.

Collective Wellbeing

Throughout the world, governments, organizations, and communities are beginning to recognize the urgency to center *collective wellbeing*; the belief that together, people, organizations, and communities can intentionally develop their highest potential and reimagine the purpose of society.

A collective wellbeing framework pushes back on outdated economic models of success — such as Gross Domestic Product (GDP) — in exchange for integrative approaches that include domains such as health, time use, community vitality, and ecological diversity and resilience.

In a university framework, the number of graduates and postdocs who receive tenure track positions is a traditional measure of achievement, along with the number of first author publications at the time of graduation. But what if we created new indicators? The reality of today's changing job market — combined with a movement toward embracing non-tenure- track careers — means that a new way of measuring success is in order.

What would doctoral and postdoctoral training look like if it centered collective wellbeing as an indicator of progress?

What if the future of graduate training considered students' perceived social support? Confidence in themselves and their potential?

Encouragement to test new ideas and learn from failure? Belief that a meaningful career was possible? Recognition as dynamic beings, with multiple identities?

Graduate programs are due to ask some hard questions about their purpose, including whether their criteria for success align with the reality of what society needs.

Though the path to change is undoubtedly challenging — even painful — universities already have the fundamental keys for transformation: brilliant minds, a passionate and dedicated workforce, a hunger for knowledge, etc. It's the scaffolding that bears reframing.

For the sake of society, doctoral students and postdocs need validation to explore their deepest sense of purpose, values, and impact. In doing so, the message is clear: Who you are — and how you make meaning in the world — matters. That's powerful.

The academy — like every institution at this pivotal moment of disruption — is due for a reckoning and a radical transformation.

In navigation, dead reckoning is how you calculate your location. It involves knowing where you've been and how you got there—speed, route, wind conditions. It's the same with life: We can't chart a new course until we find out where we are, how we came to that point, and where we want to go.
   —Brené Brown, American Social Work Professor & Author

References

1. National Science Foundation. (2020). Survey of Earned Doctorates. https://www.nsf.gov/statistics/srvydoctorates/.

2. National Academy of Sciences, National Academy of Engineering, and Institute of Medicine. (2014). The Postdoctoral Experience Revisited. National Academies Press. https://doi.org/10.17226/18982.

3. Hill, P. L., Sin, N. L., Turiano, N. A., Burrow, A. L., & Almeida, D. M. (2018). Sense of Purpose Moderates the Associations Between Daily Stressors and Daily Well-being. Annals of Behavioral Medicine, 52(8), 724–729. https://doi.org/10.1093/abm/kax039.

4. Burnett, W., & Evans, D. (2016). *Designing Your Life: How to Build a Well-Lived, Joyful Life*. Knopf.

5. Singh, D. (2018). *Purposeful Hustle: Direct Your Life's Work Towards Making a Positive Impact*. BookBaby.

6. Gallup, Inc. (2021). *CliftonStrengths Assessment*. https://www.gallup.com/cliftonstrengths/en/252137/home.aspx.

7. Connor, J. (2014). *How to Write a Personal Purpose Statement*. LinkedIn. https://www.linkedin.com/pulse/20140609202917-14809800-how-to-write-a-personal-purpose-statement/.

8. Prof2Prof. (2021). *The Higher Ed Ecosystem.* https://www.prof2prof.com/.

9. Winn, M. (2014). *What is Your Ikigai?* The View Inside Me. https://theview-inside.me/what-is-your-ikigai/.

10. Serowik, K. L., Khan, A. J., LoCurto, J., & Orsillo, S. M. (2018). The Conceptualization and Measurement of Values: A Review of the Psychometric Properties of Measures Developed to Inform Values Work with Adults. *Journal of Psychopathology and Behavioral Assessment, 40*(4), 615–635. https://doi.org/10.1007/s10862-018-9679-1.

11. Laloux, F., & Wilber, K. (2014). *Reinventing Organizations: A Guide to Creating Organizations Inspired by the Next Stage in Human Consciousness.* Nelson Parker.

12. Slade, S. (2018). *Going Horizontal: Creating a Non-Hierarchical Organization, One Practice at a Time.* Berrett-Koehler.

13. U.S. Small Business Administration. (2021). *Office of Small Business Development Centers.* https://www.sba.gov/about-sba/sba-locations/headquarters-offices/office-small-business-development-centers.

14. Wackett, K. (2018). *Be Bold. Be Brave. Be You. A Therapeutic Workbook and Coloring Book.* Kinda Creative, LLC.

15. Wheatley, M. J. (2017). *Who Do We Choose to Be?: Facing Reality, Claiming Leadership, Restoring Sanity.* Berrett-Koehler.

16. Greenblatt, A. (2000). *Work Values Exercise.* University of Richmond - Career Services. https://careerservices.richmond.edu/students/resources/pdfs/jobs-and-internships/work-values.pdf.

17. Mather-L'Huillier, N. (2021). *Non-Academic Careers.* FindAPhD. https://www.findaphd.com/advice/doing/phd-non-academic-careers.aspx.

18. Schillebeeckx, M., Maricque, B., & Lewis, C. (2013). The Missing Piece to Changing the University Culture. *Nature Biotechnology, 31*(10), 938–941. https://doi.org/10.1038/nbt.2706.

19. Skakni, I. (2018). Doctoral Studies as an Initiatory Trial: Expected and Taken-for-Granted Practices that Impede PhD Students' Progress. Teaching in Higher Education, 23(8), 927–944. https://doi.org/10.1080/13562517.2018.1449742.

20. Dericks, G., Thompson, E., Roberts, M., & Phua, F. (2019). Determinants of PhD Student Satisfaction: The Roles of Supervisor, Department, and Peer Qualities. Assessment & Evaluation in Higher Education, 44(7), 1053–1068. https://doi.org/10.1080/02602938.2019.1570484.

Acknowledgements

This book is a dream realized. It's a proclamation of self-love over fear, confidence amid uncertainty, and the belief that when we nurture our deepest sense of purpose, we give others unspoken encouragement to do the same.

To my darling and brilliant husband, Francisco, for his enduring love, enthusiasm, and commitment to co-creating the life I cherish.

To my late parents, who forever encouraged my love of learning and nourished my delight for the unconventional. Their belief in me remains a powerful source of comfort.

To my creative, compassionate, and funny kiddos, Niko and Dessa Rose, for sharing their excitement and joy. They are my light, my love, and my faith that a brighter future is ahead.

To my accomplished, devoted, and generous friends, Kerry, Linda, Gail, Tina, Sandrine, Elsa, Alicia, Samira, Dawn, Marian, Rachel G., Rachel E., JoAnn, and so many others, who encourage me to be the best version of myself by virtue of their powerful examples.

To my friend and dissertation chair, Stephanie Robert, for supporting my professional and personal evolution, sticking by me through seasons of uncertainty, holding on to a sense of wonder and curiosity, and for being the compassionate leader that Higher Ed needs.

To my friend Kristen Slack, a dynamic professor and ed-tech entrepreneur, for encouraging me to write this workbook, reading and prototyping early drafts with her doctoral students, and for being such a down-to-earth, kind, and accessible human being.

To my friend and dissertation committee member, Tracy Schroepfer, for encouraging me to apply for my PhD and for offering me loving guidance every step of the way.

To my friend and mentor, Don Coleman, for showing me the path to self-awareness, mindfulness, and joy in following my intuition.

To my colleagues, Andrew Cusick and Ellen T.A. Dobson, for their invaluable insights into the hearts and minds of postdocs, and for their feedback on early drafts of the workbook.

To the American Family DreamBank, for helping to make this workbook a reality by providing writing and coaching support and for their steadfast commitment to my career dreams.

To author Susanna Daniel, for sharing her insider knowledge of the publishing world and outstanding feedback throughout the writing of the workbook.

To Jonathan Gordon at the Research Triangle Institute for his patience and help navigating data from the National Science Foundation's Survey of Earned Doctorates.

Acknowledgements

To the PhDs who graciously shared their career stories, challenges and discoveries, may their journeys continue to light and inspire the path for others.

And finally, to you, dear readers, for your bravery to forge new paths, your dedication to science and learning, and for the remarkable ways each of you will change the world as only you can.

Biography

When it comes to creating a more just and beautiful future for all, Rebecca thrives at weaving together multiple ways of knowing. From honoring embodied wisdom, relational and cultural histories, to cutting edge theoretical and applied models of systemic transformation, Rebecca's leadership is characterized by a reverence for collective understanding. This approach has served her well navigating partnerships across academic, nonprofit, private, and government sectors.

As the Co-Director/Co-Founder of the nonprofit organization, the Institute for Collective Wellbeing (www.instituteforcollectivewellbeing.org), Rebecca brings her passion for participatory methodologies and program design, cross-sector partnership development, equity and inclusion, and a steadfast devotion to wellbeing for all to everything she does. She is also the President of Explore, Create, Evaluate Partners (www.ecepartnersllc.com) and The Purposeful PhD (www.thepurposefulphd.com) where she provides organizational and personal consultation related to purpose-driven and values-aligned decision-making.

Rebecca received her master's and PhD in social welfare at the University of Wisconsin-Madison Sandra Rosenbaum School of Social Work. She is also a board-certified coach. Rebecca lives in Madison, Wisconsin with her husband, Francisco, and their children, Niko and Dessa Rose.

www.ingramcontent.com/pod-product-compliance
Lightning Source LLC
Chambersburg PA
CBHW040424100526
44589CB00022B/2819